the outdoor
SURVIVAL
HANDBOOK

Rob Beattie

APPLE

First published in the UK in 2012 by
Apple Press
7 Greenland Street
London NW1 0ND

www.apple-press.com

ISBN: 978 1 84543 464 9

Conceived, designed, and produced by
Quid Publishing
Level 4 Sheridan House
114 Western Road
Hove BN3 1DD
www.quidpublishing.com

Printed in China

1 3 5 7 9 10 8 6 4 2

Every effort has been made to ensure that all of the information in this book is correct at
the time of publication. This book is not intended to replace manufacturers' instructions in
the use of their products—always follow their safety guidelines. The author, publisher, and
copyright holder assume no responsibility for any injury, loss, or damage caused or sustained
as a consequence of the use and application of the contents of this book.

CONTENTS

Introduction

As the gears in the urban machine grind on, many people are taking time out to rediscover their love affair with nature. For some, it's a chance to revisit a youth where hiking trips were a regular treat; for others, it's an opportunity to get acquainted with Mother Nature for the very first time.

If you want to get close to things, to get inside how they work, then you need to walk among them. Hiking – or just plain old walking if you prefer lets you do that in a way that's both recreational and responsible. It's not expensive, it's good for your health, and, done right, it has a low impact on the environment.

This book takes place in the great outdoors. Its central characters are all of us, and the action is set in some of the most beautiful and awesome landscapes on earth. The pages that follow are designed to do two things.

First, to help keep you safe, should accident or circumstance prolong your outdoor adventure for longer than you planned.

Second, to help you to be a good citizen of the woods, the mountains, the deserts, the valleys and the waterways, and to respect both fellow adventurers and the wildlife that makes these places their home.

So far as it's possible, we've made using the book a snap. It's divided into ten chapters. The first two are designed to walk you through the preparations for your outdoor adventure.

We'll tell you about the gear you need to keep warm and dry, help you put together your medical kit, sleeping, camping and navigational equipment, and advise you on the best thing to carry it all in. The chapters after that look at the difficult situations you might encounter in the outdoors—getting stuck, lost or hurt—and offer easy-to-follow, practical advice on how to stay safe, get warm, get shelter and get help.

In addition, at the back of the book you'll find our Quick Reference section, which lists common problems and then offers proven strategies and techniques for solving them—along with information on radio channels, emergency signals, conversion tables, animal tracks and a glossary of terms.

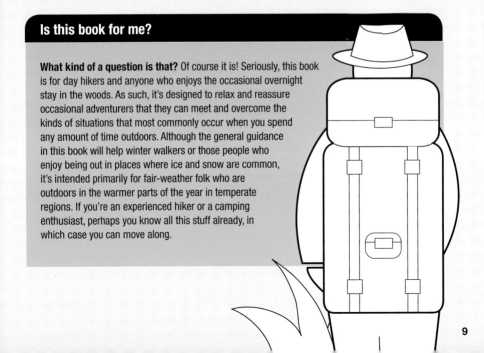

Is this book for me?

What kind of a question is that? Of course it is! Seriously, this book is for day hikers and anyone who enjoys the occasional overnight stay in the woods. As such, it's designed to relax and reassure occasional adventurers that they can meet and overcome the kinds of situations that most commonly occur when you spend any amount of time outdoors. Although the general guidance in this book will help winter walkers or those people who enjoy being out in places where ice and snow are common, it's intended primarily for fair-weather folk who are outdoors in the warmer parts of the year in temperate regions. If you're an experienced hiker or a camping enthusiast, perhaps you know all this stuff already, in which case you can move along.

1 GETTING READY

Most day hikers get in trouble for one reason and one reason alone—because they aren't properly prepared. In this chapter, we'll tell you how to get your gear—and yourself—into good shape for hiking.

Getting Ready

Getting Going

Getting Stuck

Getting Lost

Getting Hurt

Getting Shelter

Getting Warm

Getting Food

Getting Wet

Getting Help

First Thoughts

When you're planning a hike, preparation is everything, and without it you can easily find yourself in trouble. Nobody wants to be the sorry soul who the search party leads out of the woods, hungry and thirsty, sandals in shreds—yet every day people head off down the track with only the faintest idea of what they're doing. Don't let that person be you. Instead:

DO

✓ Tell someone where you're going and when you intend to be back. Arrange to check in with them.

✓ Wear sensible gear—and that includes the right kind of footwear.

✓ Carry water—you'll need about 2 litres per person per day, and up to twice that in hot weather.

✓ Prepare by walking with a loaded pack, wearing your hiking boots/shoes.

✓ Find out and fulfil local regulations regarding permits and other forms.

✓ Stick to the track if there is one. It's usually there because it's the best route.

✓ If you get lost, stay where you are.

✓ If you're in a group, stay together.

✓ Take a map and a compass, and know how to use them.

✓ Practice anything you're unfamiliar with, like lighting a fire, beforehand.

DON'T

✗ Treat a hike as if it were a walk in the park.

✗ Rearrange existing campsites.

✗ Drink alcohol.

✗ Take your pet with you.

✗ Approach or try to feed any wild animals.

✗ Drink untreated water (see pages 125–127).

✗ Leave any rubbish—pack it all out.

➤

A map and a compass are important tools. Make sure you know how to use them

THE OUTDOOR WORLD

While the practicalities of good outdoor citizenship are important, there's also more to all this than a set of rules and regulations, or do's and don'ts. So while we obviously commend the practical advice in the pages that follow, we'd also urge you to embrace the outdoors with an inquisitive mind and an open heart.

ROOM FOR ALL

You can find hiking paths and campsites to suit every taste and all levels of expertise—whether you're after the close-to-wilderness experience with no facilities other than those you provide yourself, or something slightly more civilized, where the tracks and campsites have been designed with comfort and safety in mind.

Not only can you choose the type of outdoor experience that best suits your interest, but you can change your mind as the seasons progress or as you get older. Like nature itself, hiking and camping offer almost infinite variation. The same is true for those who love the water, where there are boats of all shapes and sizes to enjoy on every kind of water imaginable—from whitewater rivers to serene, secluded lakes, and from rugged estuaries to the challenge of the open sea.

The outdoors offers a chance to escape from the cocoon of modern life and visit an alternative emotional landscape. Not only is it a place where everyone can relax and enjoy some downtime, it's an opportunity to spend time together. Relationships—whether between families, friends or partners— can be redefined and rediscovered when there are no distractions.

Tell someone what your plans are

This is the single most important rule for anyone who's going hiking, be it for a few hours, a whole day or overnight. Tell a friend where you're going and when you expect to be back. Tell them where you're going to park your car and what route you intend to take. Most important of all, arrange a time when you're going to call them to say that you've arrived back safely. If you do all this and you get lost, you can sit tight in the knowledge that when you don't make that call, someone is going to raise the alarm and you'll be found.

When you're in the middle of nowhere it really doesn't matter who makes the most money or whether the sales for that month are up or down, or if the office computer network is on the blink. Nobody has to work late, or do their homework, or get up and catch the bus; and no-one hogs the remote because there's no TV to watch.

At night, with a mug of hot chocolate in your hands, beside the still-warm embers of a dying fire and wrapped in a blanket, there are plenty of stars for everyone.

Getting
Ready

Getting
Going

Getting
Stuck

Getting
Lost

Getting
Hurt

Getting
Shelter

Getting
Warm

Getting
Food

Getting
Wet

Getting
Help

What to Wear

When it comes to clothing, think comfort, comfort, comfort. That means keeping your body at the right temperature and staying dry.

We function best at temperatures between 11 and 35°C. Most hikers favour the layering system, described opposite, because it's lightweight, flexible and easy. You can pack the same gear throughout the year, simply adding more layers in winter as required. If you're too hot, you can take a layer off and stuff it in your pack. If the wind's bothering you, the outer layer will keep it off without making you sweat. This is a much more efficient use of pack space than taking multiple T-shirts or other tops. In cold weather, thermal underwear may not be fashionable, but it is cosy.

In general, you should choose loose-fitting clothing that offers some protection against prickly plants and biting insects. Some companies offer clothing that is impregnated with insect repellent, which might be a good choice if you are particularly susceptible. Long trousers that zip off into shorts are also a useful option and will help to keep the weight of your pack down—choose ones that have a half-zip up the leg so you can lose the bottoms without taking your boots off. Finally, light-colored clothing shows up pesky insects, such as ticks, more easily so you can remove them.

What to (under)wear

While everyone agrees that chafing can stop you in your tracks as fast as a foot blister, opinions vary as to how best to prevent the problem. Loose-fitting boxer shorts have their fans, as do fitted shorts where the seam is flat-sewn and lies towards the front of the shorts. Alternatively, try cycling shorts made from Lycra.

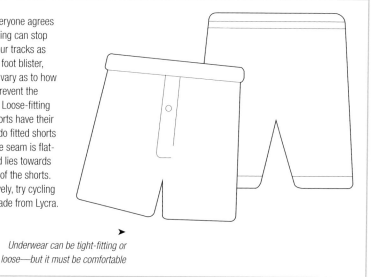

➤

Underwear can be tight-fitting or loose—but it must be comfortable

The Layering System

Clothes don't actually make you warm. Their job is rather to stop the body losing heat, which is where the layering system comes in. The concept is simple. Several thin layers will keep you warmer than one thick layer because they trap the warm air produced by your body. There are three parts to the layering system: the base layer, the insulation layer and the shell layer. All three should be breathable, so that moisture can pass through them. They should also be quick-drying.

A BASE LAYER

This must be good at removing moisture from your skin (this is called "wicking") and distributing it evenly to the surface, where it either evaporates or passes on to another layer. Base-layer clothing is typically branded as some kind of hi-tech "performance" fabric.

AN INSULATION LAYER

Usually consisting of a micro-fleece shirt or jumper, this retains body heat by trapping warm air. In very cold conditions, several loose-fitting layers will keep you much warmer than one thick one.

A SHELL LAYER

Although lightweight, windproof, and waterproof, this layer still allows moisture to escape. How? Courtesy of microscopic holes small enough to allow sweat out, but too small to let rain in.

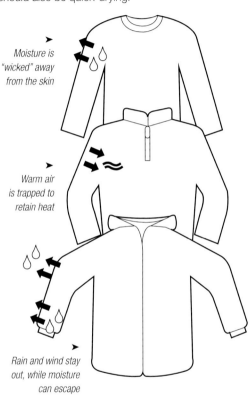

Moisture is "wicked" away from the skin

Warm air is trapped to retain heat

Rain and wind stay out, while moisture can escape

Natural v. synthetic

Ah, the old argument. Why spend all that money on fancy hiking gear when you've got a perfectly good T-shirt, a thick cotton shirt, and a pair of denims? Well, cotton is good because it breathes, but it's bad because it sucks up moisture and won't let it go in a hurry, so you can get cold even from your own sweat.

It absorbs rain in the same way, gets heavier and stays wet. Modern fabrics also absorb moisture, but usually between, rather than within, the actual fibers, so they dry more quickly and, in many cases, can actually be wrung out.

Getting
Ready

Getting
Going

Getting
Stuck

Getting
Lost

Getting
Hurt

Getting
Shelter

Getting
Warm

Getting
Food

Getting
Wet

Getting
Help

Footwear

First things first. Never set off with a new pair of anything on your feet. It doesn't matter whether they're sturdy hiking boots, high-top jungle boots, trail sandals, or trail runners—you're issuing an open invitation to Mr Blister and his pals.

Before you buy your shoes, get your feet measured properly, and when you try them on, wear the socks you're going to be using on the hike. Walk around the store and go up some stairs. Some stores have a sloping board you can try. If your toes touch the front of the shoes, they're too small. If you can feel your heel lifting at the back, they're going to give you blisters. Remember, too, that your feet are going to swell as the day goes on, so if in doubt, err in favor of one size too big.

*Light backpackers
offer good support*
➤

Broadly speaking, there are three types of hiking boots: lightweight day hikers, cut at the ankle, which are suitable for use on clear, dry tracks with a small day pack; light backpackers, which have better ankle and arch support and include a waterproof liner; and true hiking boots, which are usually made of leather, are higher-cut, waterproof and warmer. All should have solid soles that you can't twist easily in your hands.

*Hiking boots are
higher-cut and are
waterproof*
➤

Naturally, there are thousands of different kinds of boots and shoes, so take the advice of your local outdoors store and choose the ones that feel most comfortable and suit your purpose best. Remember, too, that you'll be walking with a pack of some sort—the extra weight will also influence your choice.

*Day hiking boots
are good for clear,
dry tracks*
➤

What to wear inside your boots

You'll find all manner of "technical" socks in the stores but, in reality, there's not much that can beat a pair of thin nylon socks with a decent pair of woollen hiking socks worn on top. If you want to travel light, spares are frowned upon, but two of the exceptions are underwear and socks. Nothing else will make you feel better (and cleaner) more quickly.

Accessories

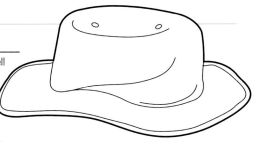

HATS

The human head doesn't work very well outdoors because it gets hot, cold and wet too easily. In cold weather, the problem is that it's radiating heat like crazy, all the time. Depending on which scientist you believe, a colossal 60 percent of your body's heat loss is caused by heat flying out through your head (and neck). Clearly this needs to be stopped in cold weather. Equally, you need to keep the top of your head and your neck protected in bright sunlight, and keep the whole thing dry if you can.

Surprisingly, a single, packable, waterproof, brimmed floppy hat (preferably with an adjustable chin strap) will do the job in most conditions for most day hikers. Remember that, like clothing, hats don't actually make you warm, they simply stop the heat escaping, so it doesn't necessarily need to be some huge fur-covered monster. The brim will keep the sun off, and hats are often more practical in the rain than pulling up the hood of your outer layer, because when you turn your head, the hat goes with you, whereas the hood usually does not.

If you prefer a baseball cap, consider one that has a drop-down "tail" at the back to protect your neck from the sun. Bandannas are good, too, because they're light, compact and adaptable (you can wear them tied round your head, over it, or as a neck flap under a cap). There is also a bandanna variation shaped like a tube, which can be worn as a scarf, hat or muffler.

GLOVES

Most of the time you shouldn't need them. When you do, go for polyester gloves that have been treated to make them water-resistant. If you think you're going to be out anywhere really cold, consider mittens instead of gloves, because they allow the air to circulate more effectively and thus keep your hands warmer.

*Bandannas—
light and
adaptable*

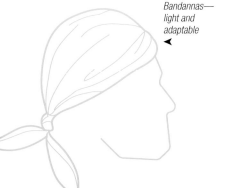

Glasses

Keep glasses in a sturdy case or around your neck on cord if you need them frequently. Consider photochromic glasses that will darken when exposed to sunlight. For very fine work, use the magnifying glass that's in your outdoor kit (pages 24–25). Polarized sunglasses cut down on glare and should be part of every hiker's kit, but avoid cheap ones because they rarely offer proper protection from ultraviolet light. Take two minutes to tighten the screws on your glasses (and everyone else's in your group) before you go.

Getting Ready

Getting Going

Getting Stuck

Getting Lost

Getting Hurt

Getting Shelter

Getting Warm

Getting Food

Getting Wet

Getting Help

Backpacks

Day hikers or single overnighters shouldn't bother with fancy external-frame backpacks with adjustable back systems. For most day hikes you won't need anything bigger than a 35-litre capacity, going up to a third more capacity if your trip is in the cooler months or if you're planning a night or two away.

Since most backpacks aren't waterproof (whose bright idea was that?), consider buying a cover or choosing one with a cover that zips away into the top pocket. In emergencies you can tie your poncho around the backpack.

Trying out a backpack is a bit like trying on a pair of boots. You should go to a proper outdoors store, explain what you want to use it for and then try several. Load each one with the weight you expect to be carrying (you can't judge the suitability of an empty backpack) and walk around the store, up and down a few stairs, take it off and put it back on again. As you do, get

an assistant to adjust the straps so that it sits comfortably on your back.

Generally, packing a backpack is common sense. Heavy items should go towards the bottom (a tarp, tent, or bedroll strapped underneath the pack can help weight distribution, too). Keep hard-edged stuff away from your back, and don't pack your toilet paper underneath everything else. That just about covers it.

HOW MUCH SHOULD YOU CARRY?

As little as possible. You can usually tell an experienced hiker by how little they have, rather than how much. As a general guide, you shouldn't try to carry more than between 25 and 33 percent of your own body weight.

Where did you put it?

Where indeed. Make the first time you have to empty your backpack in order to find something tucked away at the bottom the last time, and resolve to get organized. Keep anything you'll need during the day (or in a hurry) either near the top of your pack or in its own side pocket. Keep loose items to a minimum. Colour-code your stuff sacks so you know what's in each one. Wear a bum bag for stuff you need to get at even faster (sunscreen, insect repellent, sunglasses and so on), and once you've discovered a way of packing your backpack that works, stick to it.

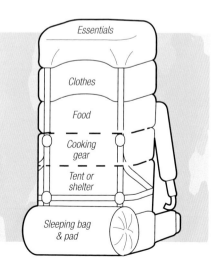

Essentials

Clothes

Food

Cooking gear

Tent or shelter

Sleeping bag & pad

A Good Night's Sleep

Tired from the trail, your body will want to sleep. However, unless you can create the right conditions, this won't happen.

First you need a sleeping bag. Get a "mummy" bag with a hood (remember all that heat radiating from your head?) and check that it's got a bit more padding than the rest of your bag. Mummy bags are more versatile, pack up smaller and generally weigh less than rectangular bags, which only come up to your shoulders. If you're buying from a good outdoors store then the quality should be fine, but check the seam stitching and the zipper.

Many bags come with a season rating, but this is unreliable because manufacturers haven't standardized the

way it's measured. Instead, look for a temperature rating — something rated at −12 to −6°C (10–20°F) will keep you cosy through three seasons in temperate zones. In high summer, a light sleeping bag will do. If in doubt, err on the side of warmth — you can make a bag cooler by opening the zipper or loosening the hood, but it's much harder to make it warmer.

The best sleeping bag is no good without some kind of sleeping pad. This not only offers extra comfort and support but also acts as a crucial insulating layer between your soft, warm self and the hard, cold ground. The self-inflating kind are excellent and surprisingly compact.

Down or synthetic?

Here's the deal. A sleeping bag filled with goose or duck down will keep you warm, packs up small and is very light—as long as you keep it dry. When down bags get wet they are very hard to dry out, especially on the track. Synthetics take up more space and weigh more, but perform a little better when damp and are easier to dry out. The trick is not to get your bag wet in the first place, so keep it in a waterproof stuff sack.

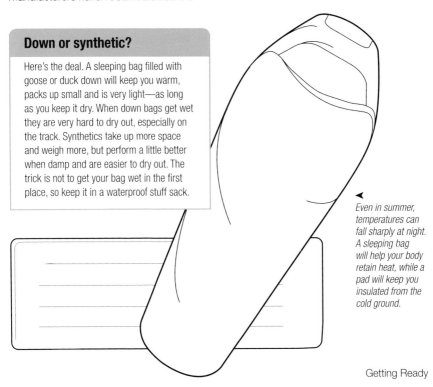

◄ Even in summer, temperatures can fall sharply at night. A sleeping bag will help your body retain heat, while a pad will keep you insulated from the cold ground.

Getting
Ready

Getting
Going

Getting
Stuck

Getting
Lost

Getting
Hurt

Getting
Shelter

Getting
Warm

Getting
Food

Getting
Wet

Getting
Help

Under Cover

If you've planned for a night out under the stars, then you'll have a tent of some description and you'll know how to pitch it. But what if you planned to stay at a shelter or hut on the trail and, for whatever reason, didn't make it? Or what if you've lost your way and need to make an unexpected overnight stop outside?

There are a number of practical shelters that are small enough for you to carry in your backpack in case of just such an emergency.

The best bivies have a "mouth" that lifts open to keep the fabric off your face and a fine mesh to keep insects out

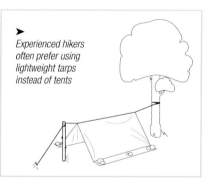

► *Experienced hikers often prefer using lightweight tarps instead of tents*

Swing low

If you're hiking in the woods, consider taking along a hammock. It'll get you off wet ground and away from nasty critters, and, once you get used to it, it can deliver one of the comfiest night's sleep imaginable. Use it under a tarp and you'll stay dry too. See the knots section on pages 100–103 for how to secure a hammock. In fact, a number of companies now sell a variety of shelters that can be suspended from trees.

BIVY BAG

Some are little more than hi-tech sleeping bag shells; others come with a pole or hoop like a mini-tent to keep the top off your head. If you don't like sleeping with something touching your face, this is a good choice, but it will weigh slightly more.

TARPAULIN

A waterproof sheet can be arranged on poles or sticks and secured with rope to provide a simple shelter.

BIVY SACK

This is essentially a large plastic bag in which you can put your sleeping bag and mat for the night.

"SPACE" BLANKET

This weighs just 50 grams or so, folds down small and reflects up to 80 percent of your body heat back to you.

LAWN AND LEAF BAG

A heavy-duty household plastic bag will do in a pinch. Take a couple so you can put one inside the other and line the space between the two with leaves for insulation.

Round the Campfire

Should you take any cooking gear with you? Obviously, if you're off on a full-scale week-long hike then you're going to need to eat something, and while the manufacturers of sealed, ready-to-eat foods suggest that you can eat them cold, straight from the packet, doing so will make meal-times a miserable affair. Unless you strive to become a one-pan gourmet, most meals will involve adding boiling water, and that means a stove. Here are your main options:

GAS CANISTER STOVE

FOR—Easy to use, steady flame, inexpensive.
AGAINST—Propane canisters are heavy, and butane doesn't burn well at very low temperatures.

LIQUID GAS STOVE

FOR—Cheap, burns cleanly, good in windy conditions and high altitudes.
AGAINST—Harder to operate, needs cleaning.

WOOD STOVE

FOR—Don't have to carry your fuel.
AGAINST—Open fires may not be allowed; what happens when it's wet or there's a solid-fuel fire ban in place?

SOLID FUEL STOVE

FOR—Comes in a pack containing fuel tablets and an ingenious fold-out metal stove—and it's tiny.
AGAINST—Very susceptible to wind.

If you're only planning for emergencies, then the solid fuel stove is your best bet. You'll also need a cooking pot (about 1 litre capacity should be enough for dinner), an insulated mug and a little knife-fork-spoon cutlery set.

Food and water

If you're actually going to cook (as opposed to reheating or rehydrating camp food), then brown rice or pasta is a good choice, combined with dried soups and sauces. When you're on the go, dried fruit, nuts and energy bars are good, or you can make your own trail mix of peanuts, dates, raisins, chocolate and so on.

Cranky-in-the-morning hikers should also remember the coffee.

Take a couple of small bottles of water (rather than one large one) because the unopened one will taste fresher. Refill it whenever you can. To save space, consider a collapsible bottle, which you can also freeze the night before for a hot day.

Solid fuel stoves are light and very reliable. The tablets can also be used as lighters.

Getting Ready

Getting Going

Getting Stuck

Getting Lost

Getting Hurt

Getting Shelter

Getting Warm

Getting Food

Getting Wet

Getting Help

Your Medical Kit

Of course, nobody wants to deal with a medical emergency on the trail, but you may be forced to, so it's best to be as prepared as possible, and that means a medical kit. There's no point including items that you don't know how to use, so keep that in mind when you're putting your kit together, and don't be seduced by all sorts of exotic medical paraphernalia. Alternatively, many outdoors suppliers will be happy to sell you a pre-packed kit that contains many of the items listed here.

Most situations you'll encounter will be minor inconveniences—cuts, bruises, stings, scrapes, blisters, chafing and so on—that can be treated with the items in the kit, but you should also buy, read and pack a good basic first-aid book. This will help you deal with unfamiliar medical situations as well as any possible emergencies. Finally, your medical kit should include a healthy portion of common sense.

WHERE SHOULD YOU PUT YOUR KIT?

Keep the medical kit stowed towards the top of your pack, so you can get to it in a hurry, or in a bum bag that you wear around your waist. Some hikers like to do both, keeping the main medical kit in their backpack and a smaller version in a bum bag, so that if they lose their pack, they've still got some basic medical supplies on hand.

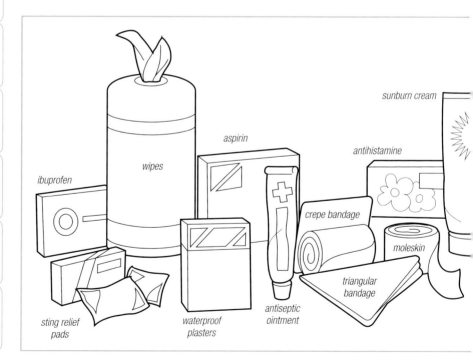

sunburn cream, antihistamine, aspirin, wipes, ibuprofen, crepe bandage, moleskin, triangular bandage, antiseptic ointment, waterproof plasters, sting relief pads

Your medical kit should contain the following:

- 2 x pairs of surgical gloves
- Antiseptic cleaning wipes
- Thermometer
- CPR mask or shield
- Pair of small scissors
- Pair of EMT Medical Shears
- Tweezers
- Scalpel
- Safety/blanket pins
- "moleskin" or "second skin"
- Sting relief pads
- Elastic bandage roll (3")

- Sterile gauze pads x 10
- Flexible splint
- Duct tape
- Triangle bandage
- Butterfly closure strips x 5
- Trauma Pad (5" x 9") x 1
- Selection of assorted waterproof bandages
- Aspirin
- Ibuprofen
- Extra strength non-aspirin tablets

- Antihistamine
- Lip ointment
- Burn cream
- Sunburn cream
- Hydrocortisone cream
- Triple Antibiotic Ointment

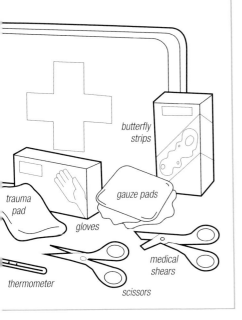

butterfly strips

gauze pads

trauma pad

gloves

medical shears

scissors

thermometer

FIRST AID

You can and should learn basic first aid and CPR (cardiopulmonary resuscitation) skills before you go on a hike, because these will help you to use the tools in your medical kit effectively. Your local Red Cross and St John Ambulance run regular first-aid courses and you should sign up for one today. They'll also have all sorts of other, more specialized, courses, but first aid and CPR are the two you need to attend.

Special medical requirements

If this is your first hike in a while, get a physical examination from your doctor. If you have a specific medical condition, whether it's hayfever or any other allergy, asthma or diabetes, find out if it's still safe to hike, and then make sure you have any treatments or medicines you might need—even if you're only going out for the day.

Getting Ready

Getting Going

Getting Stuck

Getting Lost

Getting Hurt

Getting Shelter

Getting Warm

Getting Food

Getting Wet

Getting Help

Your Outdoor Kit

The contents of your outdoor kit will dictate your level of comfort should you choose—or be forced—to stay outdoors longer than you originally intended. It should contain all the things necessary to help you prepare a warm, safe camp for the night; it should also allow you to attract attention if you get into difficulties.

Your outdoor kit should contain the following:

- Whistle
- Knife
- Waterproof/ windproof matches
- Lighter
- Magnesium fire striker
- Box of tinder
- Solid fuel portable stove
- Travel towel
- Water purification tablets/water filter
- Cord/rope/ parachute cord 15m
- Spare laces
- Bug net/bug hat
- Insect repellent
- Space blanket/ bivy sack
- Poncho

- Torch x 2
- Toilet paper
- Map & waterproof map case
- Compass
- Resealable bags
- Stuff sacks
- Paper and pencil
- Fleece-lined stuff sack (reverses into a pillow)
- Extra batteries
- Magnifying glass
- Signal mirror
- Sewing kit
- Candles
- Toiletries
- Something to read
- Spare tent stakes
- Fishing line and hooks
- Camp axe
- Folding spade

MOBILE PHONES

Considered overkill by some hikers, there's nothing wrong with taking your mobile phone with you. Make sure it's charged up, and try to find out what the coverage is likely to be where you're hiking. Don't rely on being able to get a signal and make an emergency call. If you can, it's a bonus.

TORCH

If you've got room, take two or three—a small pencil light for general use; a broad-beamed LED mini light that you can clip onto your shirt or jacket and that gives a uniform spread of light; and a headlamp for when you need to use your hands. Choose a pencil light that has a candle mode so that you can unscrew the head and the bulb will remain burning like a candle; good torches will also have a spare bulb in the tail cap. In general, ordinary torches will give you better directional light, while LEDs give good coverage and the batteries and bulbs last longer.

KNIFE

This is probably the most personal item of gear, and no-one can really recommend a knife for someone else. If you choose a folding knife, make sure it locks into position when the blade is extended and that the hinge doesn't flex too much. Experienced hikers favour straight, unflashy-looking knives without serrated edges or fancy handles. Double-edged blades are both impractical and potentially dangerous. Look for a knife with a blade about 10cm long and a sheath that holds it securely. If you've got room, a multi-tool knife (like a Swiss Army® knife or a Leatherman®) is also often useful.

FIRE LIGHTER

Ordinary matches won't cut it outdoors, buy waterproof ones, preferably in a waterproof container. It doesn't hurt to have a lighter either. And as backup, carry a magnesium fire-striker or other commercial fire starter that will generate super-hot sparks to light your tinder. If you're a complete fire klutz, a packet of fire sticks is easy to light, or use the fuel from your stove. Carry one or two packets of fast-lighting artificial tinder in case conditions are wet.

Getting Ready

Getting Going

Getting Stuck

Getting Lost

Getting Hurt

Getting Shelter

Getting Warm

Getting Food

Getting Wet

Getting Help

Navigation

No-one actually wants to get lost. In fact, on many well-maintained and well-marked trails you'd think it was virtually impossible to do so. Yet, every year, hikers stride confidently off into the distance with no clear idea of where they're going. They certainly don't have a map or a compass. This is plain dumb. Neither of these is hard to use and in fact, it's actually fun to know where you are, to see where you've been and to plan where you're going next.

COMPASS

A compass is simply an ultralight magnetic needle on a frictionless bearing that responds to the gentle tug of the Earth's magnetic field. The needle has an arrow on it that points to magnetic north, and stationed around the arrow are north, south, east and west, and a scale from zero to 360.

There are two basic kinds. The first is the kind you hold in your hand so you can quickly tell where north is—it's often combined with another tool: for example you might find one on the pommel of a knife. The second kind is often called an orienteering compass. It is mounted on a flat piece of plastic and is designed to be used in conjunction with a map. Unless you have a specific reason for doing otherwise, this is the kind you should get. We'll tell you how to use a compass, starting on page 32.

MAP

Not all maps are created equal, and there's only one kind you should use when you're on—or off—the trail. It's called a topographic map (topo for short) and it differs significantly from the other kinds.

Don't think you can use a tourist map to find your way around. These are designed to give you a general impression of the features or attractions that a particular area offers and should not be relied on. They'll help you find the car park and the restaurant, but not much else. They're often not even drawn to scale. Walking trail maps are more tempting because they look more detailed and they show the trail and some of the surrounding features clearly. Provided that you can still keep your car, the café or the gift shop in sight while you walk the track, then use one by all means—otherwise, stick to a topo map.

Various different kinds of compass are available— ask your local store for an orienteering compass

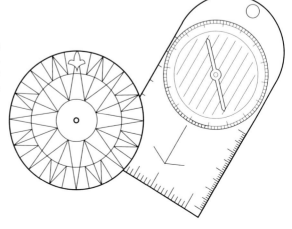

You Versus the Weather

In a straight fight, you'll always lose, so treat the weather with the respect it deserves. That means being aware of your limitations and understanding the impact the weather can have, not just on your enjoyment but on your ability to achieve almost anything outdoors.

If you've followed the rest of the advice in the Getting Ready section, you should be able to cope with the general ups and downs of getting wet and being too hot or too cold. Indeed, solving those problems is part of the fun. However, bad weather is always something to be taken seriously, and you should always check the forecast in the days before you start your trip.

If you're planning to hike locally, then TV, radio station and newspaper reports will keep you up to date. Check the five- or seven-day forecasts so you don't have any nasty surprises on longer trips. If you are traveling somewhere else to hike, you'll need to find some way of getting the forecast for your destination. For National Parks, there's usually plenty of information available by telephone or via the internet.

One last thing—hiking after dark is a risky business, so make sure you know what time the sun sets.

Knowing the weather forecast can make all the difference between a good trip and a miserable one

Ponchos

Speaking of bad weather, spare a thought for the humble poncho, because it could be one of the most practical pieces of gear you pack. Even an inexpensive poncho will do the job of keeping you—and your pack—dry and well ventilated. Then, with some rope and a bit of ingenuity, it can be turned into a simple shelter from either the sun or the rain (see page 93).

2 GETTING GOING

Hiking is supposed to be fun, so don't muck it up for yourself by not knowing where you're going, and don't muck it up for others by being inconsiderate. OK. Told everyone where you're going? Arranged to call someone when you get back? Got your medical kit and other outdoor gear? Practised important skills such as putting up your tent or your tarp and fire lighting? Got yourself in shape? Pack firmly on your shoulders? Let's get going.

Getting
Ready

Getting
Going

Getting
Stuck

Getting
Lost

Getting
Hurt

Getting
Shelter

Getting
Warm

Getting
Food

Getting
Wet

Getting
Help

Solo Camping

Although solo camping is common, there's a prevailing view that you shouldn't hike on your own. There are good reasons for this, but in truth they apply mainly to solo hikers who like to get out into the wild and really test themselves against the elements. For our purposes, the worst thing you're likely to experience in a campsite or on the trail is a touch of loneliness, and there are plenty of ways around that.

ARE YOU LONELY TONIGHT?

If you're camping alone, think about the kind of campsite you want to stay at and how long you want to be there. The notion of getting away from it all for a week by a remote lake might sound like a good idea, but are you the kind of person who will run out of things to do the minute you've set up your tent?

WHERE ARE YOU?

If you're planning a solo camping trip, perhaps with a bit of hiking thrown in, tell someone when you're leaving, where you're going, and when you expect to get back. Arrange a time to check in with them on your return and consider calling them during the course of the trip to let them know everything's fine. If you're staying in a supervised campsite, make sure that you give them the campsite's contact details, and be sure to let them know if you change your mind and go somewhere else instead. If you're in camp and decide to go off for the day, find the people running the camp—and maybe a friendly neighbour—and tell them. Give them your mobile phone number if you have one; also take theirs.

If you're determined to go it alone:

* Take things to keep you company—books, an MP3 player (one that runs on standard batteries is better, because you won't need to recharge it), music and audiobooks.

* Find things to do—fishing, sketching, painting, writing or animal watching.

* Learn to play a musical instrument. There are lots of inexpensive travel guitars (these have smaller bodies than usual); the recorder and fiddle are good; the harmonica is fabulously portable and supremely atmospheric.

* Keep a journal.

* Practise everything at home first—pitching the tent, lighting the stove, purifying water and so on. You'll really appreciate the effort once you're there.

What Makes a Map?

We've already talked about the kind of map you need, but it's worth repeating. Tourist and walking trail maps are no good—you want a proper topographic map that shows you the actual shape of the land. This will give you a clear idea of which way to go, how far away things are, where you can find water, where there's a campsite, where the land slopes steeply and will mean you're in for a hard climb, and where you can look forward to a more leisurely stroll. Topo maps do this by using contours—imaginary lines that link together a series of points that are the same height (or elevation) above sea level. Lines that are close together indicate a steep slope; lines further apart a more gentle one.

Map symbols and features will include:

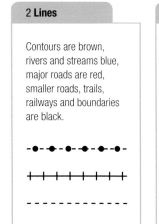

1 Areas

Vegetation is green, water is blue and information updated from the last edition of the map is in purple.

2 Lines

Contours are brown, rivers and streams blue, major roads are red, smaller roads, trails, railways and boundaries are black.

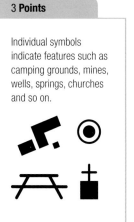

3 Points

Individual symbols indicate features such as camping grounds, mines, wells, springs, churches and so on.

All of these symbols will be explained in the map key on your particular map.

Hike with a friend

It's more fun outdoors if you've got someone to share it with. You will get a helping hand when there is something to overcome, companionship when there is something to enjoy, and a shoulder to cry on when there isn't. Unless there is a specific reason to do otherwise—such as in a teaching situation, for example—try to go with someone who is at the same overall fitness level as you and who has similar hiking experience. One of the biggest causes of trouble on the trail is when a slower partner is struggling to keep up with someone who is more able. If you do hike alone—and many people do—then make sure you fill out the relevant forms where required. And you did tell someone where you were going, didn't you?

Getting Ready

Getting Going

Getting Stuck

Getting Lost

Getting Hurt

Getting Shelter

Getting Warm

Getting Food

Getting Wet

Getting Help

Your Map and Compass

The first rule, if you're on a path, is to stick to it. The people who made it probably knew what they were doing. If you lose the path, then you can use your map and compass to find it again, or reach your destination another way if you must.

First, though, you need to make the connection between the map and the actual landscape around you. Start by finding some landmarks, such as a range of hills, a lake or a river. Then try to find them on the map. Given that you ought to know roughly the direction in which you're heading, it shouldn't take too long to get the map facing the right direction. Hold it flat in front of you and turn yourself around until you can match up the real features in front of you with their equivalents on the map. Keep in mind that contour lines that are close together indicate ground that is steep. By checking the contour lines and using the other symbols on the map (see page 31) you'll be able to orient yourself quite quickly.

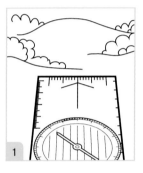

1

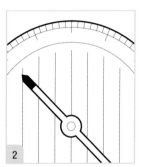

2

3

1 Let's say you're heading for that hill in the distance. Get your compass out and point the direction of travel arrow at the hill.

2 Wait for the magnetic needle to settle.

3 Turn the dial (also called the bezel) until the marker for north lines up with the magnetic needle. This is called setting a bearing. If you keep the needle lined up with north and always follow the direction of travel arrow, you'll eventually arrive at the hill. Even better, you'll stay on course even when you're at the bottom of a thickly wooded valley and can't actually see the hill. That's because knowing where north is and following the direction of travel arrow will keep you on course.

That tricky North Pole

There are actually two North Poles: the magnetic one that your compass points to, and the geographic one that your map says is north. The difference between the two— which can be as much as 30 degrees—is called declination. The actual value of this will be expressed on your map as either a westerly (negative) or easterly (positive) declination. For example, if you're heading along a bearing of 90 degrees, but your map tells you there's a declination value of −10, then you're actually heading along a bearing of 80 degrees. In order to correct your course, you'll have to set your compass to a bearing of 100 degrees. Even a small declination can put you kilometres off course if you don't compensate.

USING THE MAP ON ITS OWN TO NAVIGATE

OK, but what happens if you can see where you want to go on the map but can't find it in real life—maybe because it's hidden behind a bank of fog, because darkness is falling or because it's somewhere over a few ridges? As long as you know where you are and where you're going on the map, you can use that and the compass together to plot your course without being able to see any of the landmarks in real life. Here's how it works:

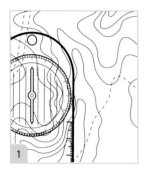 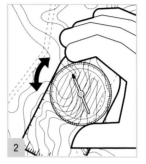 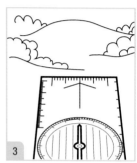

1 Imagine a straight line on the map between where you are and where you want to go. Lay the compass on the map so that its long side is on this line.

2 Turn the housing until the north marker is pointing to north on the map (north is usually at the top).

3 Lift the compass off the map and then turn it until the needle lines up with the north marker on the housing. The direction of travel arrow will now show you which way to go.

Map scales

The scale of the map you buy is very important, but because it involves figures, many of us switch off. Here's what you need to know. For actual hiking, your map should be at the following scale:

* 1:24,000—where 1cm represents 240m (1in represents 2,000ft)
* 1:25,000—where 1cm represents 250m (1in represents 2,083ft)

For planning a longer hike, try:

* 1:50,000—where 1cm represents 500m (1in represents 4,166ft)
* 1:100,000—where 1cm represents 1km (1in represents 1.6 miles)

The smaller the number after the ":" sign, the more detail the map will show. If you're planning a significant hike, it may be best to have a map with a 1:50,000 or 1:100,000 scale so you can see the whole trip, but then have several maps at 1:25,000 so you can see the route in more detail.

Getting
Ready

Getting
Going

Getting
Stuck

Getting
Lost

Getting
Hurt

Getting
Shelter

Getting
Warm

Getting
Food

Getting
Wet

Getting
Help

Show Some Respect

Although the great outdoors is a symbol of freedom, like all freedoms it comes with a price tag: rules. Many of these are unwritten, common courtesies that fellow travellers should automatically extend to each other and to their surroundings. Many, however, are written down. It's your responsibility to make sure that you know what the rules are and to follow them.

Each park or trail system will have its own individual rules and regulations that responsible hikers are expected to obey. The exact rules will vary depending on where you are, but you can expect them to include:

- No alcohol.
- No fires (or local campfire restrictions may apply).
- No collecting of firewood.
- Make sure fires are properly extinguished.
- No camping outside of established sites or in certain restricted areas.
- Dispose of washing water responsibly.
- Use permanent toilets where available.
- Bury human waste.
- No glass bottles or containers.
- Hunting by permit only, at specific times.
- Snares or traps are forbidden.
- No pets, or pets only allowed in certain areas.
- Hikers must stay on the trail.
- Do not shortcut across hairpins.
- Hikers must obey signs indicating private property.
- Don't leave any rubbish—if you can carry it in, you can carry it out.
- Observe all posted signs.
- Do not feed wildlife.
- Plants and rocks are not souvenirs.
- Look after your children.
- Be quiet at night.
- There are special regulations regarding public water supplies.
- All relevant permits and forms must be completed.

How much does it cost?

Although camping permits are required for many National Parks, they are usually free. However, on some well-used tracks you may have to pay to use one of the provided shelters. Some parks also require you to reserve your permit in advance—so check before you travel.

Basic Trail Etiquette

As well as obeying the rules regarding the environment, you should also be considerate of your fellow hikers. Although these rules aren't necessarily written down, they've evolved to create an informal code of conduct that helps everyone—experienced hiker and newcomer alike—to get along.

Follow these simple rules and you won't go far wrong:

- Respect the rights of other trail users.
- If you're in a group, travel in single file so you don't widen the trail.
- Walk through small obstacles like puddles—stepping around them widens the trail.
- Don't block the trail so that others can't get by.
- If the trail is blocked by an object that you can move, do so. If you can't, note the location and report it.
- Don't surprise someone that you need to pass. Let them know you're coming.

- If you meet someone coming towards you who's slower than you, stand aside and let them pass rather than making them wait.
- Conversely, let faster hikers pass you.
- Be aware that the trail may be shared by cyclists and horse riders. The rule here is that hikers give way to horses and that cyclists give way to hikers and horses.
- Horses can be nervous, so take care if you find yourself sharing a trail with them. Move to the lower side of the track if you can. Talk quietly.
- Downhill hikers give way to uphill hikers.
- Don't remove or change trail signs.

Leave No Trace

Getting Ready

Getting Going

Getting Stuck

Getting Lost

Getting Hurt

Getting Shelter

Getting Warm

Getting Food

Getting Wet

Getting Help

In recent years, outdoor activities like hiking, cycling, climbing and off-roading have reached new levels of popularity. Inevitably, with more and more people spending time in the outdoors this has placed increasing pressure on natural habitats and the environment in general. In response, a number of organizations and codes of conduct have developed in order to protect the outdoors and promote respectful attitudes among those using it.

A number of environment-conscious organizations have created codes of conduct that promotes hikers and off-roaders to enjoy the outdoors more responsibly. One of the most significant is Leave No Trace, a nonprofit association with a presence in Australia, New Zealand, Canada, the United States and Ireland. Its seven principles are simple:

• Plan ahead and prepare.
• Travel and camp on durable surfaces.
• Dispose of waste properly.
• Leave what you find.
• Minimize campfire impacts.
• Respect wildlife and farm animals.
• Be considerate of other visitors.
In other words, good common sense,

Burying human waste is considerate and better for the environment ➤

and the sort of principles that any modern-day hiker should be eager to embrace, whether you're a hardened ultralight backpacker or a family day-tripper.

RUBBISH

No-one wants your rubbish—not even you—but since you brought it with you, behave responsibly and take it away again when you leave. If you've planned your trip properly, you shouldn't generate huge amounts of rubbish anyway, so pack it away in a few plastic bags and dispose of it (or, better still, recycle it) at home.

GOING TO THE TOILET

If you need to go for a pee, step off the trail and into the bushes so you can do it in privacy without offending others or embarrassing yourself. If you need to have a poo, you should use a trowel to dig a hole about 15cm (6in) deep and at least 100m (300 odd ft) away from the trail, your camp or water. Toss in the toilet paper and fill in the hole when you've finished.

CAMPFIRES

The best way to minimize the impact that fires have on the environment is not to light one in the first place. Instead, use a lightweight stove to cook with and lanterns for light. If you want to light a fire, first make sure it's permitted. Second, use existing fire rings, pits or pans and keep the fire small. Only use fallen wood (if permitted), burn everything to ash, extinguish the fire, and, once they are cool, scatter the ashes.

MAKING CAMP

Actually, that should be "Not Making Camp," since you should always try to use a campsite that's already there in preference to making a new one. Don't "improve" an existing campsite by clearing the ground or cutting back tree branches and bushes, and don't spread out unnecessarily—a good campsite is a small one. If you must make a new camp, set up at least 30m (100ft) from water and out of sight of the trail. And if you want to stay more than one night, move camp slightly the next day to minimize your impact. When you leave, it should look as though you were never there.

WASHING DISHES

The eco-friendly way to wash your dishes is to fill a cooking pot or collapsible bottle with water, and use biodegradable soap detergent. Don't simply rinse things out in a stream. In fact, do your dishes well away from water sources—at least 50m (150ft).

Leave no trace

Do:

✓ Familiarize yourself with the rules and any special concerns about your destination.
✓ Avoid busy times, and travel in a small group.
✓ Use established paths and campsites, and camp at least 50m away from streams and lakes.
✓ Take rubbish, leftovers and anything else with you when you leave, or deposit it in the bins provided.
✓ Use a stove for cooking and a candle or torch for light.
✓ Respect other campers and hikers —let them enjoy their outdoor experience as well.

Don't:

✗ Create your own campsite or try to "improve" existing ones.
✗ Spread out your campsite unnecessarily.
✗ Touch rocks, plants or other natural features.
✗ Bring non-native species with you °into a new area—they can spread pests and diseases.
✗ Approach or feed an animal—it changes their behaviour and feeding habits, and may endanger their health.

Getting
Ready

Getting
Going

Getting
Stuck

Getting
Lost

Getting
Hurt

Getting
Shelter

Getting
Warm

Getting
Food

Getting
Wet

Getting
Help

Pacing Yourself

So you've hit the trail full of good intentions. You know how to read a map and use a compass, and you fully intend to leave no trace of your passing. There's just one important thing left that all hikers have to master—how to pace themselves.

The classic mistake is simply to set off too quickly. This is understandable. You're probably excited or you may not have much time on the trail that day, or you may feel that it's not "proper" hiking if you don't raise a sweat almost immediately (and, of course, many people hike specifically to lose weight). Only you can find your own pace. When you do, it'll be the speed at which you can walk all day without actually getting tired. Sure you'll feel a few aches and pains, but you won't suffer from the dog-tiredness that says you've been hiking too hard. If you're traveling in a group, the slowest person needs to set the pace—and

that means putting them at the front so they don't get left behind. This may be frustrating for faster, more able members of the group, but it's the safest way to proceed and, over time, the overall speed of the hike will increase as everyone's fitness levels gradually improve. (And if you followed our advice back on page 31, there shouldn't be too much difference in the fitness levels of group members.)

KNOW WHERE THE EXITS ARE

Don't be a martyr. If you're struggling with the pace of the hike, or your new boots are giving you blisters, or your pack's not set or loaded right, or you've just plain had enough, then bail out. There are usually a number of different points along the trail where you can return to civilization and get a well-earned breather or a hot cup of coffee. If you're in a group, let the leader know and then arrange where and how you're going to rejoin to the hike later.

HELPFUL HINTS

If you're all bundled up, remove a layer before you start—otherwise you may end up sweating too soon; by the same token, monitor your body temperature so you can add or remove layers if necessary, so you stay comfortable. The good news? You should snack regularly, especially if you're not used to hiking, because this will keep your energy levels up; and of course, drink plenty of water so you stay hydrated. If the pace of the group is slow because you've got members who aren't used to hiking, you may find that more experienced hikers feel more tired at the end of the day. That's because it's more difficult

If you can walk and talk at the same time, you've found a comfortable pace ➤

walking at someone else's slow pace than it is walking at your own natural pace.

WHAT MAKES A GOOD PACE?

That depends. It depends on the terrain, the conditions, your size and weight, how much you're carrying, your level of fitness, and, importantly, how tired you are. You may be super-fit, but your pace will slacken if you're walking over sand or gravel, or into a head wind, or the light is fading and it's hard to see where you're going. An average hiker—as if there is such a thing—should be able to walk at between 3 and 5km/h (2–3mph) on firm, flat ground, with a pack. It's difficult to give further advice, but the rule of thumb says that if you can walk and talk at the same time without getting out of breath, then your pace is about right. If you become breathless, you should slow down. Once you've got an idea of your average speed, you can use it to estimate how far you'll travel in a day. Bear in mind, however, that you'll be doing other things on the trail apart from walking—stopping

for lunch or to take photographs or go to the toilet, or just pausing to admire the view. Factor these pauses in when you're estimating trip times. You may also find a pedometer useful, as it will help you keep track of how you're doing minute by minute and allow you to adjust your pace accordingly. It also gives you a great sense of achievement as you watch the kilometres – or miles – ticking away.

Trekking poles

Although some hikers consider them an affectation, trekking poles do have their advantages. They make life easier going uphill or downhill, they allow you to test in front of you for swampy ground, and two poles used together will reduce the amount of stress you place on your knees. A single pole is more useful in helping you to keep your balance over difficult terrain. Poles can also be used with a tarp or poncho to make a shelter. Light poles are best, but they cost more.

3 GETTING STUCK

Imagine the scene. You're enjoying an afternoon's hike when you hit really muddy ground and suddenly everything takes twice as long; or a summer storm sweeps in and you have to wait it out under cover; or you simply aren't able to walk as far as you thought you could in a day. Changes of terrain, unexpected ugly weather, failing daylight—welcome to the wonderful world of getting stuck.

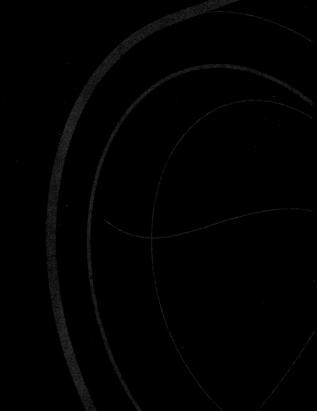

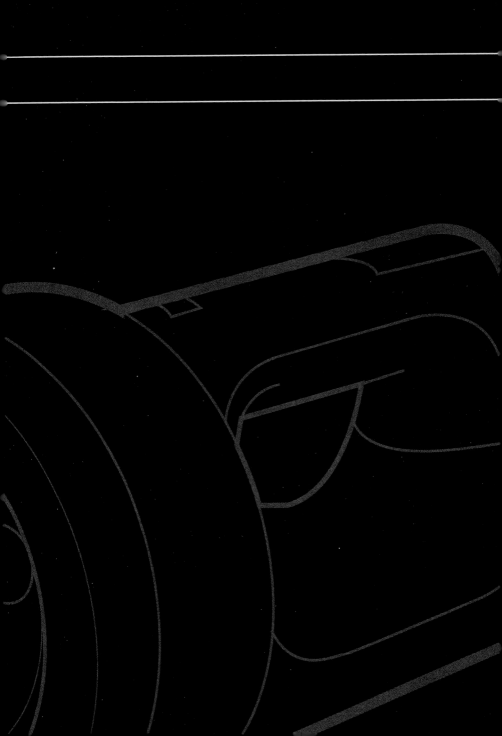

Getting Ready

Getting Going

Getting Stuck

Getting Lost

Getting Hurt

Getting Shelter

Getting Warm

Getting Food

Getting Wet

Getting Help

Watching the Weather

A cloudy sky doesn't always mean it's going to rain, but how can you tell the good clouds from the bad ones? By knowing a little bit about the different kinds of cloud and understanding what they tell you about what's going on in the atmosphere, you can make some fairly accurate predictions.

CIRRUS

Typically found at above 5,500m (18,000ft), these are wispy and thin, and mean that there's moisture high in the atmosphere. They often indicate the end of fine weather.

CIRROCUMULUS

Found above 5,500m (18,000ft), these are little rounded white puffs of rippling cloud. Like cirrus, they often indicate the end of fine weather.

ALTOCUMULUS

Usually found at 1,800–6,000m (6,000–20,000ft), these are little white puffs of cloud that can gather in clumps or fill the sky. They may mean that rain is on the way. Otherwise it's likely to become overcast.

ALTOSTRATUS

Usually found at 1,800–6,000m (6,000–20,000ft), these cross the sky in layered dark gray sheets. Although you may see the sun through them, they indicate that there's lots of moisture in the air, and rain is on the way.

STRATUS

Usually found below 1,800m (6,000ft), these are solid grey clouds that fill the sky and often appear vague and fog-like as they can form just above the treetops. Stratus clouds often bring a light mist or persistent drizzle that can be a problem.

STRATOCUMULUS

Low-lying clouds, usually found below 1,800m (6,000ft) with a solid base and often occurring under storm clouds (cumulonimbus), they look more threatening than they actually are. Expect light rain, sleet or snow depending on the temperature; can indicate bad weather that's either on its way or just clearing.

CUMULUS

Usually found below 1,800m (6,000ft), these look like the kind of clouds that kids draw and tend to signify good weather. However, if the atmosphere becomes unstable, they can also appear as vertical clouds that may develop into cumulonimbus.

CUMULONIMBUS

These are vertical clouds that can start very low, at around 300m (1,000ft), but can rise to form colossal columns more than 18,000m (60,000ft) high. They nearly always mean trouble in the form of thunderstorms—sometimes very powerful and violent ones—with heavy rain, hail or sleet.

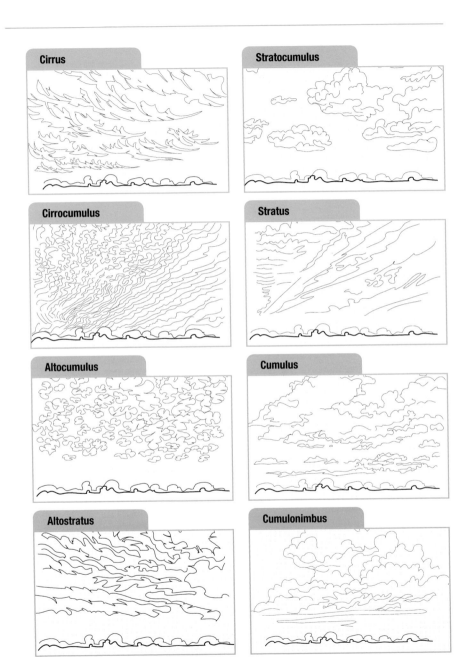

Cirrus

Stratocumulus

Cirrocumulus

Stratus

Altocumulus

Cumulus

Altostratus

Cumulonimbus

Getting Ready

Getting Going

Getting Stuck

Getting Lost

Getting Hurt

Getting Shelter

Getting Warm

Getting Food

Getting Wet

Getting Help

Watch Out!

Getting stuck isn't like getting lost. Often, when you're stuck you know exactly where you are. You can point to yourself on the map and say "I'm right here." The trouble is, you're supposed to be somewhere else—meeting someone back at the camp or going out to dinner. Instead, you're here, and unfortunately, you're stuck.

To avoid getting stuck, you should always keep an eye on the following:

WHAT'S THE WEATHER DOING?

A sudden storm can drive you under cover or make the trail too treacherous to walk safely.

WHAT'S THE TERRAIN DOING?

Use your map to anticipate changes in the conditions that may affect your walking speed and slow you down. Ask hikers coming in the opposite direction what the trail ahead is like.

WHAT'S THE LIGHT DOING?

If you know when the sun sets and know how fast you're walking, you should be able to make a judgment about whether you're going to finish your hike as planned. There's nothing wrong with bailing out earlier than you'd planned. No-one wants to hike in the dark, so avoid it if at all possible.

However, so long as you've prepared properly, being stuck is OK. You can spend the night and then make your way out the following morning in daylight. If you have a mobile phone and you can get a signal, call the person you're supposed to be meeting and let them know you're fine, just temporarily delayed. Then turn to page 91 and find out how to set up your camp.

If you run out of daylight, don't try to walk out. Hiking in the dark is just plain dangerous—even with a good head lamp—and you shouldn't attempt it unless you absolutely have to (see page 48). When you can't see properly, all the potential dangers around you become magnified, and it's easy to trip and twist an ankle, slide down a slope or turn yourself around so you're lost as well as stuck.

WHAT ARE YOU DOING?

Let's face it, nature is such a glorious companion that it's easy to get distracted and lose track of time (or even doze off after a hearty lunch). The best way to ensure you don't get stuck is to stay alert—you can still enjoy what's going on around you and still stay on track.

◀ *Staying aware of what's happening around you helps you anticipate potential problems*

Lightning

Why does lightning occur? Particles in the clouds become charged (no-one agrees exactly how) so that the top is positive and the bottom is negative. This generates a similarly segregated electrical field. As the storm increases, a positive charge builds up in the earth under the clouds—it's at its most concentrated in tall objects such as trees. Once the negative and positive charges in the cloud and the ground have reached a certain level, an electrical discharge passes between the cloud and the earth as a lightning bolt. It's more complicated than that, but you get the picture. More to the point, a single lightning bolt can be 8km (five miles) long, carry 100 million volts of electricity and generate temperatures of 27,000°C (50,000°F). Respect.

Now, the chances of being struck by lightning are pretty slim—between 1 in 280,000 and 1 in 700,000, depending on whose figures you believe—but who needs that kind of action? Here's what you need to know about lightning and how to avoid getting hit:

- Lightning can strike many kilometres away from any rainfall.
- Darkening cloud bases and rising wind are danger signs.
- If you can hear thunder, a lightning strike is possible (even in clear skies).
- Sound takes about 3 seconds to travel 1 kilometre. Light takes no time at all. So if you see lightning and hear thunder 15 seconds later, it's only 5km away and you need to take action.

- Head for a permanent shelter or a metal-roofed vehicle (but don't touch the metal once you're inside).
- Get rid of your pack and dump any other metal objects (pole, knife etc).
- Don't stand near a single tall object such as a tree, because lightning prefers tall things and can also "jump" to nearby objects—such as you.
- Don't stand near anything metal—like a wire fence or railway line.
- If you're in a wood, find a group of trees and stand in the lowest spot.
- If you're in the open, squat down.
- If your hair stands on end or your skin tingles, crouch on the balls of your feet, put your head between your knees and fold your hands over your head, to make yourself small and minimize your contact with the ground.
- Sit on a foam pad if you've got one.

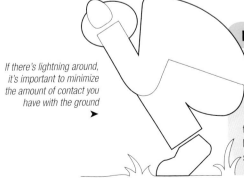

If there's lightning around, it's important to minimize the amount of contact you have with the ground
➤

If lightning strikes...

The most common injuries from a lightning strike are burns and shock, but people can also die, either from respiratory or cardiac arrest. As with all serious injuries, call the emergency services if you're able to—if not, check for a pulse at the neck or behind the knee. If you can't find anything, start CPR (see page 76).

Getting Ready

Getting Going

Getting Stuck

Getting Lost

Getting Hurt

Getting Shelter

Getting Warm

Getting Food

Getting Wet

Getting Help

Terrain

Apart from the weather, the other major factor that causes people to get stuck is changing terrain, sometimes combined with changing weather conditions. Don't forget that, although you may have missed a particular rainstorm, you might find yourself walking into an area that it did hit and having to cope with the aftermath.

Watch out for the following:

MUDDY GROUND

A sudden storm or a flash flood can turn even a well-established trail into a slippery ribbon of mud. Hiking through mud is hell. To stop yourself from slipping you will tend to shuffle or plant your feet down flat instead of walking with your normal stride. This uses your muscles and joints—especially the knees—in weird and uncomfortable ways. You'll get tired more quickly and your boots will lose their grip as the soles become clogged with mud.

ROCKY GROUND

If you're picking your way across fairly flat ground covered with rocks of various sizes, some of them are going to be solid, some will teeter and others will slide. Since you don't know what any individual rock will do, you develop another weird walk as you try to anticipate and compensate for whichever way the rocks might behave. Going uphill is worse, with the added concern of slipping back down again.

UNSIGNED FOREST TRAILS

Of course, you shouldn't be off the main track anyway, unless you know what you're doing, but now that you've made that mistake and come this far, you'd better watch out. The floor is a minefield of nature's "gotchas," from fallen branches to dense vegetation, trailing vines and partly exposed roots. As always, the best advice on going off-track is not to. Avoid doing so unless you absolutely have to.

Waiting it out

Although your raingear ought to be good enough to keep you dry while you hike, there's no doubt that during periods of very heavy weather you should consider waiting it out, especially if there's any form of shelter nearby. If you're on a well-travelled trail, check your map and see if there are any permanent shelters marked. It is worth hiking the extra kilometre in poor weather if you know there's somewhere to rest up and dry out at the end of it. Consider turning back to find a shelter if you have to.

Other Hazards

Depending on where and when you're hiking, you may encounter one or more of the following:

FLASH FLOOD

This hard-to-predict hazard can be a killer. It occurs when a heavy storm breaks over mountains, dumping lots of water very quickly. Runoff from the torrential rains pours into valleys and gullies and forms walls of water that can be metres high. Hikers are routinely shocked by the force of flash floods. All you can do is avoid deep valleys and dry washes when it's stormy, and if it starts raining heavily, make for high ground. Be aware that it doesn't have to be raining where you are for a flash flood to affect you.

ROCKFALL AND LANDSLIDE

These are usually caused by heavy rain over time, changes in the groundwater level and fierce or prolonged cycles of freezing and thawing. (Sometimes, they're even caused by the boots of thousands of hikers going where they shouldn't.) Existing falls should be negotiated with care, since they're likely to be exceedingly unstable. You should also report them. If you're unlucky enough to be there when it happens, "Rock!" is the universal warning cry.

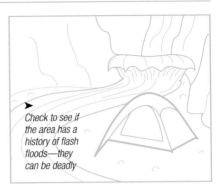

Check to see if the area has a history of flash floods—they can be deadly

SNAGS

This doesn't mean the minor things that catch on your jacket. Snags are dead trees that are still standing. They may have been burnt, or infested and killed by insects such as the gypsy moth. Over the years they lose their branches and their roots slowly die and although the reamining tree looks solid enough, it an toppled over at any time. Keep well clear.

ICE CHUTE

This can occur when snow melts and then freezes again, coating the sides of ravines and gullies with a slick surface of ice that's almost impossible to cross safely, even with crampons and an ice axe. Because they are often protected from direct sun by overhangs, ice chutes can persist even in mild weather. Only mad people believe that ice chutes are fun things to slide down.

Anticipation

Just as climbers are supposed to look a few handholds ahead, so hikers need to anticipate what is further along the trail. You can do this in two ways. First, in clear conditions where you can see ahead a good distance, use your eyes—you should be able to tell where the terrain changes appreciably and then take measures to compensate for this. If you can't see far ahead because you are hiking in a forest or because the weather is foggy or it is getting dark, then you will have to use your map and your common sense.

Moving in the Dark

Getting
Ready

Getting
Going

Getting
Stuck

Getting
Lost

Getting
Hurt

Getting
Shelter

Getting
Warm

Getting
Food

Getting
Wet

Getting
Help

Night walking tips

Because of the way the human eye works, your peripheral vision is better at night than your normal "straight-ahead" sight, so looking sideways at something sometimes gives you a clearer view. If you have a hiking pole, use that to feel for obstacles in front of you; baseball caps are also useful, especially in wooded areas because they can warn you if you're about to get poked in the eye by a low-hanging branch. Finally, refer to your map more often than you would in daylight, as you're more likely to get lost.

The first thing to say is that you shouldn't try to walk in the dark. Doing little chores in an established campsite with your head lamp on, or even making your way to the toilet, isn't the same as moving through unknown territory at night. Even established trails can kick up all sorts of obstacles that may be easy to navigate by day, but become real tripper-uppers at night.

Here's what to do if you have to move at night:

- Don't move any further than you have to. If you're moving to get out of danger, go only as far as you need to so that you're safe.
- The same thing applies if you're moving to attract attention.
- If you have no source of light, do not move unless you absolutely have to—use your hands and feet, keeping three out of the four in contact with the ground the whole time.
- Never attempt anything that would be tricky during the day—it will be many times harder at night, even with a good torch.
- If you're in a group, make sure you hold hands in such a way that you can walk in single file.
- If you have rope (you did bring rope, didn't you?) use that to keep everyone together.
- If you're in a forested area, looking up at the treetops (where it's lighter) may help you to find clearings.
- Talk to each other as you walk, and reassure any nervous members of the group.
- If you're alone and nervous, talk to yourself—if nobody hears you, who cares? If they do, then you've been rescued!
- Don't be too alarmed by noises— everything sounds louder at night.
- Listen for the sound of water, but never try to cross a river at night unless you have to.

WHITE LIGHT, RED LIGHT

Around the campsite, an ordinary torch is fine, but if you have to move at night then you'll really appreciate the headlamp we recommended back on page 25—partly because it keeps your hands free for holding a trekking pole, or your neighbour's hand, or grabbing onto something if you trip, and partly because it may come with a red light as well as the conventional white one. Red lights are much better for moving in the dark because they help preserve your natural night vision. It works like this. The retina at the back of the eye is made up of "cones", which you use for daylight vision and "rods", which you use at night. The rods can't see the colour red and so using a red light leaves our natural night vision unaffected (if you shine a white torch into someone's face it'll take about 30 minutes for their full night vision to return). Thus, a red light is much better for moving around in the dark.

THE CARROT MYTH

Sadly, while carrots are full of dietary fiber, antioxidants, and minerals, they don't actually help you see in the dark. This urban myth was put about by the Royal Air Force during the Second World War to explain why they were enjoying such success during night air battles, and was actually used to disguise advances in radar technology and the use of red lights on instrument panels.

Wait a minute

When darkness falls, at first it's important that you do nothing and let your eyes become accustomed to the dark—you will be pleasantly surprised at what you can see, even on a very dark night. Look all around you carefully. It may be that you can see a light—perhaps from another backpacker or a permanent campsite or even a building. Either try to attract their attention (see page 152) or sit tight and move towards them at first light.

4 GETTING LOST

We usually get lost not because nature performs some sneaky about-face in order to fool us, but because we stop paying attention to what's going on around us. We get over-excited about the views, or over-tired, or we muck around or get too absorbed in one thing (usually ourselves or the people we're with) and then before we know it—bang. Lost. Here's how to get lost—actually how to avoid getting lost—and then get found again.

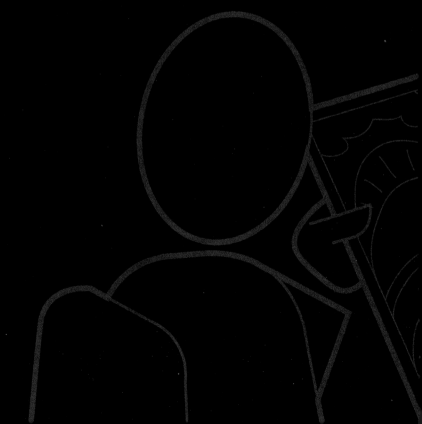

Getting
Ready

Getting
Going

Getting
Stuck

Getting
Lost

Getting
Hurt

Getting
Shelter

Getting
Warm

Getting
Food

Getting
Wet

Getting
Help

How Not to Get Lost

Nobody likes being lost. We don't even like being lost in a car, let alone out on the trail, where accidentally setting off in the wrong direction can take hours to correct—always assuming you can spot where you took the wrong turn in the first place.

The key to staying found is to use your map properly and to be aware of your changing surroundings. Spend time with your map before you set off, and then refer to it often.

Here's what to do in order to avoid getting lost:

- Before setting out, take time to study your map and plan your route. Identify features such as ridges, cliffs and river crossings, as well as possible campsites. Discuss the route with group members so that everyone knows where they're going and how they're getting there.
- When you reach the trailhead, open the map so the part you're viewing roughly coincides with the real landscape in front of you. Take some time to orient yourself and pick out any visible major features before you set off. Identify them on the map. Take a compass on overnight hikes and on any walks where the route may be less than clear.
- Unless you are very experienced, stay on the trail. Obvious? Yes. Does everyone do it? No.
- As you travel, keep the map in a waterproof map case hung around your neck, together with a notepad and a pencil (pencils work better outdoors than pens).
- Use the notepad and pencil to make a note of landmarks

as you pass them, together with the distance travelled and the time. This will help you if you need to backtrack. It's especially important to mark junctions where the trail divides, in case you take the wrong turn and need to go back.
- As you walk, refer to the map and compass every 15 minutes or so to make sure that you're still on the right track. Checking the map like this in relation to what's around you helps you build a mental map of your surroundings.

Shortcuts

The quickest way to get lost—especially in the woods—is to take a shortcut. As soon as you strike off and lose sight of the track, you're laying yourself open to getting turned around. Although you can use your map and compass to find your way back to the trail, it's just extra trouble that you don't need.

- Use the features of your map to make sure you're on the correct trail—if the contours of the map suggest you should be going down but you're still climbing, maybe it's the wrong trail.
- If the path becomes fainter and occasionally runs under low-growing vegetation, you may have inadvertently turned onto a trail made by wildlife, which could be heading anywhere—another reason to check your map every so often.
- Take a moment to stop and look behind you every now and again to get a rough picture of what the path will look like when you're coming back. It can look very different.
- If landmarks suddenly seem to be in the wrong place, check that you haven't rotated the map by 90 or 180 degrees—sounds stupid, but it does happen!
- "Navigation fatigue" can set in late in the day, and mistakes may be made. Always have frequent rest stops and try not to hike for too long in a single day. In a group, it's also a good idea to share navigational duties.
- Aim for a good, steady pace that all group members can stick to. That way, no one will fall behind.
- If you're in a large group, two people should be assigned to keep the party together—the leader and a "back-marker", who brings up the rear and ensures that no one is left behind. The back-marker role is particularly important when the leader is preoccupied by navigational duties.
- Try to form an idea of your average speed so that you can estimate how far you've tavelled and how long it will take

to get to particular landmarks ahead of you. This is a difficult art and needs practice. See page 39 ("What makes a good pace?") for more information.
- Global positioning systems (GPS) are very useful in providing navigational help, but they should not be considered a substitute for skill with a compass and map—for one thing, batteries run out; for another, they don't work in all terrain, particularly in mountainous country.

Track markers

Always keep an eye out for track markers. Worldwide, it's common practice in many parks to have tracks marked permanently with different styles of blazes. Some use painted marks, others prefer fixed plastic, metal or wood markers; some use small piles of stones called cairns, while a few use cuts made into tree bark.

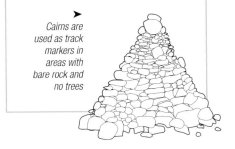

➤
Cairns are used as track markers in areas with bare rock and no trees

Getting
Ready

Getting
Going

Getting
Stuck

Getting
Lost

Getting
Hurt

Getting
Shelter

Getting
Warm

Getting
Food

Getting
Wet

Getting
Help

The S.T.O.P. Principle

There are different kinds of lost. The first kind is where you're only lost temporarily, for a few minutes or even hours, before you get your bearings again. Then there's the other kind of lost, which is a bit more tricky.

Your best chance of making sure you only ever experience the first kind is to admit you're lost early on (many people find it exceptionally hard to do this) and then apply the S.T.O.P. principle.

S **Sit.** Stop what you're doing. Don't walk any further. Admit that you're lost.

T **Think** about the last time you can remember when you knew your location—the last place that you actually knew where you were. If it's close by or you're supremely confident that you can backtrack there, then head for that spot. Otherwise, stay where you are. Think about the items you have in your backpack and how you might have to use them. If you've come prepared, this will reassure you.

O **Observe.** Look around. Get your map and compass out, check your notepad for the written record of the trip so far, and see if you can work out where you are. If there's higher ground close by (really close by—you don't want to get more lost), go up and take a look. You may be able to find yourself again quite quickly.

P **Plan.** If you're definitely lost, you can't backtrack, and there's no obvious way to find out where you are, stay calm. The best plans are made by calm people.

Never trust anyone

Be your own boss. Use your head, use your map, and when someone else says they know a great shortcut to this fabulous view that no-one knows about, use your head again. If you can find it on the map and see how to get there and back safely, then fine. If not, forget it—relying on someone else to remember how they got somewhere and then have them explain it to you is another quick way to get good and lost.

Similarly, if you're hiking in a group, don't rely on the leader. Sure, you should let them lead, but that shouldn't stop you from using your own map and compass so that you know where you are.

▲
Admitting you're lost is sometimes the first step toward finding yourself again

First Response

Once you've established that you are genuinely lost, there are four things you should do right away (assuming neither you nor anyone else in your group is hurt or in danger).

DON'T PANIC

In stressful situations, the body's natural reaction is to panic. This does all sorts of stupid things to your brain. First, it stops your body from thinking about long-term survival and gets it thinking about short-term survival—running away. This is the so-called flight response, and it can literally have you running in circles looking for a way out.

The panic state releases adrenaline, increases your blood pressure and accelerates your breathing. If you feel yourself sliding toward panic, take ten nice, slow deep breaths, counting them out each time. Repeat this a couple of times and you'll feel the panic pass. It really works.

LISTEN

When your breathing's slowed a bit, cup your hands behind your ears and listen carefully. It really amplifies the sounds around you, and you may find that you can actually hear someone else, even if you can't see them.

MAKE SOME NOISE

It may be that, although you're lost, there's actually someone—perhaps lots of people—over the next hill. It's just that at the moment you can't see or hear them and they can't see or hear you. If you have a whistle, use that. Blow three blasts and then wait, another three blasts and then wait. Repeat. This is a widely recognized distress signal. If you don't have a whistle, bang something using the same three-pause-three-pause pattern. Cooking pots can make a lot of noise. Otherwise, shout "Help!" in the same pattern.

GIVE YOURSELF A BOOST

Have something to eat and drink. Seriously. Drink some water and eat something small, like an energy bar, some trail mix, or a piece of fruit. In stressful situations your body needs energy to stay calm and focused on the task at hand, so do yourself a favor.

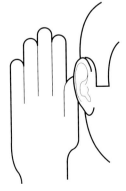

➤ *It may look stupid, but cupping your ears like this will amplify the sounds around you*

Admit you're lost

Unbelievably, some hikers refuse to admit they're lost—especially if they're supposed to be in charge of a group. This is genuinely dangerous. When people are under pressure and feel that they need to be decisive, they can strike off with apparent confidence in entirely the wrong direction. It's important, therefore, that no-one accuses a group leader or other more knowledgeable hiker of "getting us lost." Instead, try to relieve the tension, because they're still your best chance of getting found, or making yourselves comfortable for a night outside.

Getting Ready
Getting Going
Getting Stuck
Getting Lost
Getting Hurt
Getting Shelter
Getting Warm
Getting Food
Getting Wet
Getting Help

How to Find Yourself Again

So, you're still lost and there isn't anyone over the next hill who's about to come and rescue you—what's next? Continue trying to attract attention to yourself while you try the following. Bear in mind that the last thing you want to do is make things worse, so do not attempt any of these measures unless you're certain that you can do so safely, without further endangering yourself or others. If you have any doubts at all, do nothing. Sit tight. Wait for help to come to you. OK?

- If you've got a mobile phone and can get a signal, use it to call for help. Don't be embarrassed and don't put it off. Electronic devices go wrong in the wilderness all the time, and a phone that's working now may not be working in three hours' time.

- Find some high ground. Take everything with you if you're on your own, because you don't want to be separated from your gear. If you've already made a camp with a tent, bivy, tarp or other portable shelter, do not abandon it. Pack it up and take it with you. Lost hikers have been known to try and scout the area around their tent—even a brightly coloured tent—and never find it again. If you're in a group, work out

a method by which whoever goes up the hill can find their way back to the group. You can rope group members together, position them at 30-meter intervals so they can see each other clearly, tie plastic sheeting to trees where the main group is staying—anything to prevent the person going up the hill from getting separated from the group. If you can't work out a safe way to do this, don't send anyone. Instead, sit tight and wait for rescue or all go together.

◄

The higher you can get, the more likely you are to recognize landmarks that may identify your location

- Once you're up high and have a good view of what's around you, take your compass and find north. Then find north on the map, take a deep breath, and start trying to orient yourself.
- When you know which way is north and you know which way you and the map are facing, try to find some landmarks. The easiest ones to spot are high ground, valleys, lakes and rivers —unless you get lucky and see a town.
- Try not to be deceived into recognizing a landmark that's not actually there. Sometimes people get more lost because in their eagerness to "find" themselves, they mistake an unknown landmark for one that they know, and end up following a false trail.
- Look and listen for signs of other hikers in the area. Get your group to stay quiet for a few minutes while whoever is on high ground listens for the noises of a camp or other people on the track. Check for smoke signals from any nearby campfires but ensure that they're close enough so you can judge exactly where they are—you don't want to go striking off after distant smoke that's been blown in from kilometres away or that might have disappeared by the time you reach it.
- If you can't find any of the landmarks on the map, use your notes to retrace your steps from the very beginning. That may help you to locate where you are.
- Once you've found out where you are, use your map and compass to make your way—carefully—to the nearest marked trail or other sign of civilization.
- Let's say it again. Unless you are absolutely convinced that you've found yourself again and can continue with complete confidence, then stay exactly where you are, continue to make noise, and let help come to you. Remember that a search will start at the place you were last seen. If you move on, you're only moving further away from the spot that will be searched first. The only exception to this rule is if there is higher ground nearby, where you stand a better chance of being seen—and can see rescuers as they approach.

Lakes all look alike

Close up, bodies of water have a tendency to look the same. Features such as bays and inlets that may be very distinctive from the air (or when looking at a map) are so large on the ground that you may not be aware of them. It's also much more difficult to judge distances across water, so it's harder to judge the size of a lake. This can result in serious confusion. You may think you've found the large lake on your map that has a river running out of it that you can follow, but in actual fact you're looking at a much smaller lake with no river and you're about to waste valuable time and energy going off on a wild-goose chase.

No Map, No Compass

Getting Ready

Getting Going

Getting Stuck

Getting Lost

Getting Hurt

Getting Shelter

Getting Warm

Getting Food

Getting Wet

Getting Help

By now you've realized that it wasn't a very sensible thing to come on this hike without a map or a compass. You thought a quick glance at the tourist map in the shop would be enough. You won't make that mistake again. However, your one minute with the map did tell you something—that the track runs south to north and that the last few kilometres run beside a river that eventually leads down into a lake near some huts. So if you could just figure out where north is...

Finding direction with a watch

1 Hold your watch flat in your hand, face upward.
2 Point the hour hand toward the sun.

3 Find the halfway point between the hour hand and 12 o'clock on your watch.
4 In the northern hemisphere, the halfway point will be due south.

Northern Hemisphere
Once you've pointed the hour hand at the sun, you'll find due south between it and 12 o'clock. (Your watch must be set to Standard Time.)

Southern Hemisphere
Make sure that 12 o'clock is pointing at the sun and then find the point midway between it and the hour hand—that will point north.

DIGITAL WATCH

It doesn't matter if your watch has no hands. Get a page from your notepad and draw a clock face. Fill in the numbers, note the time, and place the hour hand in the proper position on the paper (or just do it in your imagination to save paper). South is halfway between the 12 o'clock and the hour hand.

Finding direction with a stick

1 Put the stick into the ground as straight as you can. Note where the end of its shadow falls and mark its position.
2 Wait for about half an hour and mark where the end of the shadow has moved to.
3 Draw a line between the two marks.
4 Bisect it with another straight line at right angles; this line runs north to south.

Finding north at night

1 Find the North Star. It is halfway between Ursa Major (the Big Dipper) and Cassiopeia (which looks like a big W). Both of these are visible year-round—assuming the night is clear. If you can't find it, imagine a straight line that starts with the last two stars at the side of the Big Dipper. Follow that imaginary line up, and the first bright star you come to is the North Star (see illustration 1).

2 Imagine a line that points straight down from the North Star to the Earth. North is where the line meets the horizon (see illustration 2).

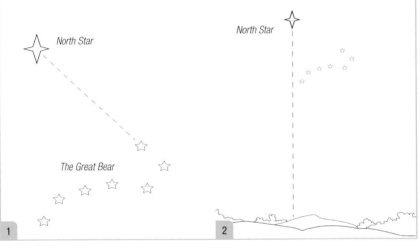

▲ *Sailors have used the stars to navigate for years. If you can find the North Star, then you can find north, whether you've got a compass or not.*

NAVIGATION MYTHS

There are lots of old wives' tales about land navigation that people should know better than to believe, including:

- Moss grows on the south side of trees and rocks (it does, but also on the north, east and west sides).

- Trees grow thicker foliage on the south side (subject to so many conditions and variables as to be untrue).

High noon

Here's a quick way to find north. If you position a straight stick in the ground at 12:00 noon, the shadow will point north in the northern hemisphere and south in the southern hemisphere.

How Search-and-Rescue Teams Work

Getting Ready

Getting Going

Getting Stuck

Getting Lost

Getting Hurt

Getting Shelter

Getting Warm

Getting Food

Getting Wet

Getting Help

Of course, you being lost is the most important thing currently going on in your world, but in the outside world things will be moving differently. Remember that a search and rescue will not start right away. You have to be reported missing first, and then the authorities have to determine whether the situation is serious. Search-and-rescue teams have been dispatched into the wilderness while the "missing" backpacker was comfortably asleep in a local motel or scanning the menu in a restaurant somewhere and wondering what all that commotion was outside.

Every team works differently, but the process will go something like this:

- Someone will miss you and you'll be reported overdue. If nobody's going to miss you because no-one knows where you are, then you're in trouble—go to page 62.
- Once the authorities are satisfied that it's a rescue situation, the search team will assemble. These are mainly volunteers and it will take a few hours.
- Once the team is together, they need to establish your likely whereabouts based on whatever evidence they can collect from your car (if you have one) or maybe from what you said to friends or neighbours.
- The first searchers will try to move quickly and head for the location where you were last seen or any known shelters in the area.

◀

Leaving clues will make it easier for rescue dogs to find you

- A search in bad weather will take longer to organize and execute. You may be cold and wet, but try to be patient.
- The searchers will make a point of checking open areas to which you may have moved in order to be spotted more quickly.
- First searchers make a lot of noise. Listen out for them and attract their attention using the three whistles-pause-three whistles distress signal or any other means of making a noise.
- Air searchers may follow. Attract their attention using the methods described on page 150 and following.
- Dogs and handlers may also take part in the search—leave clues for them, especially if you have to move, as described on page 152 and following.
- Searchers may also wait at natural boundaries such as fire breaks, rivers and streams, in case you're trying to walk out.
- For your part, don't move unless you have to. A moving target is much more difficult to find than one that's sitting still. Take all the measures you can, and then sit it out.

Common mistakes

Rescue organisations list the following common mistakes made by hikers. Said one official: "When people do get lost, it basically comes down to lack of preparation, experience, equipment and judgement."

- Inappropriate footwear
- Lack of a map
- Inadequate water supplies
- Injury or illness
- Miscalculating the time to complete the hike
- Trapped by bad weather
- Not recognizing that they are lost

It takes time to assemble a rescue team, so be patient and sit tight ➤

Getting Ready

Getting Going

Getting Stuck

Getting Lost

Getting Hurt

Getting Shelter

Getting Warm

Getting Food

Getting Wet

Getting Help

If You Must Move

As we've said repeatedly, the best advice in this situation is to stay exactly where you are or move to higher ground nearby and stay there. However, there may be situations where you feel that you have to try to find your own way out—with or without a map or a compass. Think carefully about your situation and decide whether moving will make it better or worse. Do not move unless you are convinced that things will improve, or because staying where you are will endanger yourself or a member of your group. Only move as a last resort. If you must move:

TRY TO HEAD DOWNHILL

It's by no means certain, but statistically you're more likely to hit civilization by following the landscape down. People tend to settle, cultivate and generally carve up the landscape starting at the bottom—so that's where they're most likely to be. Even if you get to a place long abandoned by people, you may still find the remnants of the trails they used that you can follow out.

FIND A RIVER

Generally you'll achieve this by going downhill. If you find running water, follow it downstream. If it joins a bigger river, follow that downstream too. It may flow into a lake where you may find a lodge or evidence that people visit there from time to time. Do not cross rivers except in a real emergency. They can be extremely dangerous, and crossing a natural barrier like a river may take you out of a designated search area.

It's a big place, outdoors. Don't move unless you absolutely have to

Walking out

One of the few instances when you can walk your way out of trouble when you're lost is if you know—absolutely know—that it's only a few kilometres to some form of civilization. Even then, you should only attempt it if you're certain you can travel in a straight line by using your map and compass or one of the methods described on pages 58–59. How is it possible to get lost when help is so close? Who knows, but people still do it. Stay calm and don't be one of them.

FIND A TRAIL

Wooded areas, especially, can change greatly, and even in a single generation trails are made, used, abandoned and neglected, rediscovered, and then used again. If you find an old disused path, then it's possible it will lead to a newer one that is more frequented. If you come across a path like this, should you turn left or right? Try the downhill route first, but watch carefully—if the path starts to deteriorate, turn back and go the other way.
Leave yourself trail markers so that you can find your way back easily.

MARK YOUR ROUTE

If you do decide to try and walk out, mark your route. Remember that search-and-rescue teams may have a pretty good idea of where you are when they start searching, and if you move you're just creating additional problems. There are many ways to mark a trail, from making stone cairns to blazing marks on trees.

TRY TO FOLLOW THE RIDGES

This is the rule in higher, wooded country. Being high up has several advantages. It makes it easier for aerial rescue parties to find you (even ground search parties can see you better at a distance) and it gives you a better view of your surroundings, raising your chances of spotting a landmark or something that you can match up to your map. If you have to spend a night outside, however, drop down from the ridge a little to get out of the wind—it'll be easier to keep warm.

Foraging?

If you're lost in the woods or the wild, and running low on food, hunger may tempt you to think that you can live off the land by collecting edible plants. Although hundreds of plant species are edible, you can't just eat any old tuber or berry-like fruit. Many plant foods are poisonous or simply distasteful; some may need cooking, for example, to remove toxins. The best advice is not to risk it. Although hunger pangs will be hard to ignore, you can survive for several weeks without food. It's much more important to stay hydrated.

5 GETTING HURT

Although it's possible you'll be one of the fantastically unlucky few who get struck by lightning, bitten by a snake, or crushed beneath a falling tree—perhaps even hit by a meteorite—most accidents in the wild are more mundane. Nonetheless, if you're far from home, even a minor mishap can quickly assume major proportions. Here's our practical guide to avoiding getting hurt and what to do if such a misadventure happens to you.

Getting Ready

Getting Going

Getting Stuck

Getting Lost

Getting Hurt

Getting Shelter

Getting Warm

Getting Food

Getting Wet

Getting Help

Why Do People Get Hurt?

Acts of God aside, most accidents are caused by inattention. When people don't think carefully about what they're doing, they make mistakes. There are various reasons for this, but the main ones are undoubtedly:

TIREDNESS

We don't think as fast or as fluently when we're tired. It's easy to misjudge distances, take more risks, refuse good advice and make decisions that are just plain bad.

OVERCONFIDENCE

You have to know what you're capable of and accept what your limitations are. Hikers can get hurt when they try something that exceeds their experience or their natural ability.

FOOLISHNESS

Nobody wants to spoil anyone's fun—that's what being outdoors is all about—but horseplay can transform the trail's natural characteristics from challenges into sources of genuine danger. Many hikers have fallen into this trap by becoming over-physical with each other or over-competitive as a group.

LACK OF ANTICIPATION

You can become so fixed on the ground in front of you—particularly on a long hike—that you don't notice what's going on around you. It's not just about walking into trees, although, heaven knows, people do. It's more a matter of being unaware of how the trail, the terrain or the weather is changing.

HUNGER OR THIRST

If you don't put the right things into your body, you won't get the right things out of it. Dehydration is a particular problem (and not just in summer) but, overall, food and drink are important for keeping your energy levels up and your mind focused on the job in hand.

Hiking and horseplay don't mix
◄

Blisters and How to Avoid Them

Although blisters are one of the most common problems you'll encounter on the trail, they're also one of the most avoidable. The important thing is to take action early, because untreated blisters will not only stop you in your tracks—they can be excruciatingly painful—but they may become infected, requiring further treatment from your doctor when you get home.

WHAT CAUSES A BLISTER?

It's usually friction between ill-fitting footwear and your foot. You can avoid this problem by breaking in your boots properly before you go hiking (see page 16). It can be exacerbated if your feet are sweaty or your socks are damp.

WHAT IS A BLISTER?

Friction damages the skin cells, which release histamine, which in turn forms a fluid sac designed to protect the new skin growing underneath the problem area. The trouble is that new skin is still tender and, should the blister burst, it can become infected

WHAT ARE THE EARLY SIGNS?

A tingling or a sense of heat from a particular area means a blister is on the way.

TO BURST OR NOT TO BURST?

If you can protect the blister, it's best to let it heal by itself, because that's what your body is trying to do. If it's gone too far, heat the needle from your sewing kit until it grows red. Let it cool, pop the blister close to its edge along the bottom (rather than in the middle) and drain the fluid. Don't remove the blistered skin, as this acts as a natural bandage. Apply antiseptic cream and dress it.

Now what

If a blister hasn't formed, cover the "hot" area with either a product like surgical tape or "moleskin" to decrease the friction. If it's starting to form, make a hole in several layers of "moleskin" the same size as the blister and then pack this around it.

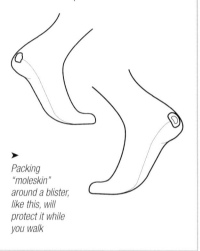

➤ *Packing "moleskin" around a blister, like this, will protect it while you walk*

BLISTERS ON YOUR HANDS

These days, many of us don't use our hands for much physical work, apart from carrying the shopping to the car once a week. If that sounds like you, then take care of your hands while you're outside, because they'll probably blister more easily than your feet. If you're not used to chopping wood, then take it easy. Don't walk with your thumbs stuck into your backpack straps, and just be generally aware that you may be using your hands in different, repetitive ways that may cause a blister.

Getting Ready

Getting Going

Getting Stuck

Getting Lost

Getting Hurt

Getting Shelter

Getting Warm

Getting Food

Getting Wet

Getting Help

Cramp and How to Avoid It

You won't die from muscle cramp—you'll just feel as if you will, particularly when an attack starts. Like blisters, cramping is almost wholly avoidable.

WHAT CAUSES CRAMP?

Either your muscles aren't getting enough oxygen or they're not getting enough water and salt.

WHAT IS CRAMP?

Apart from that agonising pain in your leg? Well, the muscles in your body flex and contract in order to move your joints. Cramp occurs when the muscle spasms in a contracted state.

WHAT ARE THE EARLY SIGNS?

Not many. You may feel a tightness in a particular muscle.

HOW TO PREVENT CRAMP.

Do some gentle stretches before you start your hike—this is especially important if you haven't hiked for a while. Eat and drink little and often to keep hydrated and energized. Try to stick to a steady pace and take short, regular rests of, say, ten minutes every hour. If you sweat a lot, try to replace what your body's losing with something salty, such as salted peanuts.

Now what?

If you get a cramp, gently flex, stretch and massage the affected area—this will get the blood back into the cramped muscle. If it's in your leg, sit down to do this. If it's in the calf, get someone else to lift your foot off the ground by the heel and gently push your toes towards you. If you're on your own, flex your foot towards and then away from you. After a while, you should be able to stand up and then gently walk the cramp off. Drink some water as well.

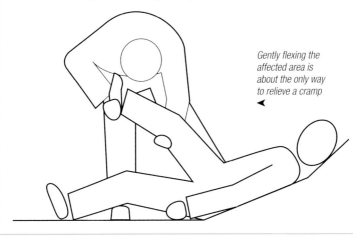

Gently flexing the affected area is about the only way to relieve a cramp ◄

Bites and Stings

Insects are everywhere, and it's much easier to prevent them from drinking some of your delicious blood, or just taking out their aggression on your delicate epidermis, than it is to treat the aftermath. Prevention, in other words, is better than cure.

- Use insect repellent. Unless you have a specific reason for doing otherwise, use a repellent that contains a high concentration of DEET, as experience shows this is most effective way of deterring common pests such as mosquitoes and ticks.
- Don't over-apply repellent, and don't get it near your eyes, your mouth, or any wounds or irritated skin. Don't apply it under clothing. Pump sprays and aerosols tend to give a more even covering than roll-ons or creams. If you're sweating a lot, remember to reapply the repellent.
- Finely woven clothing is good protection and, although less comfortable in hot weather, long-sleeved tops and long trousers also help. Some specialist manufacturers make clothes that are impregnated with insect repellent.

- Light-coloured clothes make it easier to spot small insects, such as ticks, so you can squash them. In tick-infested areas, wear long trousers tucked into socks.
- Don't sit directly on the ground or on logs, walls and so on. Ticks don't fly or jump, and can only attach themselves to you through direct contact.
- Check for ticks at the end of the day. Use fine-tipped tweezers to remove any that you find, and then disinfect the wound.
- Insects are most active from spring through to early winter in temperate areas; in a given day, they're more common at sunrise and sunset. They also love water, so observe the Leave No Trace principles and don't camp near water.
- Make sure your shelter has some kind of fine mosquito netting to keep out tiny, biting insects.

How to remove a bee sting

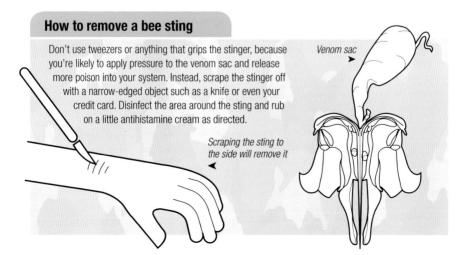

Don't use tweezers or anything that grips the stinger, because you're likely to apply pressure to the venom sac and release more poison into your system. Instead, scrape the stinger off with a narrow-edged object such as a knife or even your credit card. Disinfect the area around the sting and rub on a little antihistamine cream as directed.

Venom sac ►

Scraping the sting to the side will remove it ◄

Getting Ready
Getting Going
Getting Stuck
Getting Lost
Getting Hurt
Getting Shelter
Getting Warm
Getting Food
Getting Wet
Getting Help

Bruises and Cuts

Dealing with abrasions and knocks outdoors just takes common sense.

- Bruises are produced when the tiny blood vessels beneath the skin's surface are broken by an impact. This causes small amounts of blood to seep out under the skin. The result is the tell-tale black-and-blue markings that usually look worse than they actually are. They can still be sore though, and if that's the case, try elevating the affected area. Dipping it in cold water also helps.

- Cuts often stop bleeding on their own, but if they don't, hold a bandage or other clean cloth over the wound and apply steady, gentle pressure until the bleeding stops. Clean the wound with water that's been sterilized with iodine tablets (follow the instructions that come with them), but don't use soap. Apply some antiseptic cream and then cover the wound with a dressing. You should try to change it once a day, or more often if it gets dirty or wet.
- If it's a serious cut, turn to page 80.

Troublesome Plants

Most plants won't hurt you unless you try to eat them when - unless you know what you're doing - you're quite likely to make yourself sick. However, there are one or two plants that can make life unpleasant when you're outdoors.

- **Stinging Nettles** These are covered with tiny prickly hairs that snag your skin and then sting and itch. The hairs lay in groups, so you'll often exhibit what looks like a rash. If you wash the affected area immediately with water, the sensation will pass wuickly; you won't experience real discomfort unles you fall into a patch of nettles while wearing your swimming costume - best avoided.

- **Giant Hogweed** Popular with the Victorians (who liked their plants big) this member of the carrot family contains a toxin that can cause swelling, blisters and even burns that may scar. It's not widespread and it's hard to miss - giant hogweed can grow 4.5m (15ft) tall, it has a thick purple stem and the white blossoms can be 30cm (1ft) wide.
- **Brambles and thorns** These can do you a surprising amount of damage, especially if you go crashing through the undergrowth. Wearing long trousers will help protect your legs.

Burns

There are three kinds of burns: superficial, partial thickness and full thickness. Superficial burns affect only the top layer of skin, and may be caused by sunburn or by spilling a cup of hot coffee on yourself. Partial-thickness burns cause the skin to become raw and blistered; these are not dangerous unless a large area (more than 50 percent in adults) is affected. Full-thickness burns damage not just the skin but also fat, muscles and nerves, and as a result, the skin may appear charred.

Treating burns

- Minor burns should be treated by applying lots of cold water for at least ten minutes; remove anything from the affected area that may constrict it in the event of swelling, and then cover it with a dressing from your first-aid kit. If you don't have anything handy, you can even use a clean plastic food bag.

- Severe burns are a different matter, and there's not really any treatment you can apply. First, there's a danger of shock, particularly if the burns are extensive; second, there's a danger of infection, especially if you burst blisters or further damage the wound. Apply plenty of cold water, then lay the person down and try and make them comfortable, if you can do this without damaging the affected area. If anything is stuck to the burn, your instinct will be to remove it—don't. Obtain medical help immediately.

- If you suspect shock, try to make the person warm, raise and support their legs, loosen tight clothing, and try to keep them still while you get help.

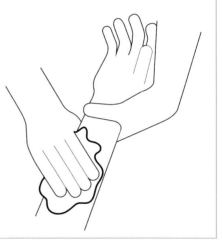

SUNBURN

There is, of course, one type of burn that you can easily prevent—sunburn. If your planned hike is in an open, exposed area, try to time your hike for the morning and evening, and find some shade when the sun is at its fiercest. Always apply sunscreen (and re-apply it every two hours), and wear loose clothing and a hat with a wide brim; and although it's irritating for them, people with fair skin or red hair need to be especially careful. If you do get sunburn, you can get instant relief by applying cool water to the burnt area; a cool gauze padding can be applied as well, but do not use any ointments or lotions. The burning feeling will persist for a day or two and you may be uncomfortable at night.

Getting Ready
Getting Going
Getting Stuck
Getting Lost
Getting Hurt
Getting Shelter
Getting Warm
Getting Food
Getting Wet
Getting Help

Hypothermia

Hypothermia is a killer. Worse still, it's a misunderstood killer, because people believe that it only strikes when it's extremely cold. That's not the case. In fact, if the other conditions are right, you can suffer from hypothermia even when outside temperatures are as high as 20°C (68°F).

WHAT IS HYPOTHERMIA?

Simply put, it's a condition that occurs when the body is losing more heat than it can generate. The body likes to operate at 37°C (98.6°F), and a slight drop of only about 2°C (3.6°F) can produce mild hypothermia.

WHAT CAUSES IT?

Apart from when it's very cold, the best—or rather, worst—conditions for hypothermia are when it's wet and windy, since this will carry heat away from the body very quickly. As water evaporates on your body it reduces the temperature of the skin, and any movement of the air speeds up the whole cooling process. If you fall in a river, you can become hypothermic within minutes—though it may take longer depending on the temperature of the water and the overall conditions.

WHAT ARE THE SYMPTOMS?

Mild hypothermia is characterized by shivering (which is what happens when your body tries to get its muscles to generate heat) followed by multiple low-level changes in behaviour. You may become irritable and less coordinated, your speech may slow or become slurred, and you'll usually become tired and lethargic. It's pretty obvious when someone is severely hypothermic. They become irrational and argumentative and may not be able to stand. Later, they may even appear to be dead.

Hyperthermia—overheating

Your body works hard to cope with heat. The blood vessels increase in size, blood flows nearer to the skin (that's why people go red in the face when they're hot), your heartbeat increases, and you sweat; the evaporation of sweat from the skin is the body's most effective cooling mechanism. If you start to feel hot and uncomfortable, it may be hyperthermia. Find some shade, sit down, rest, fan your face, take your hat off, and cool your forehead with a wet cloth.

PREVENTING HYPOTHERMIA

It's much less trouble to prevent hypothermia than it is to treat it. Following these simple rules will help:

- Stay warm and dry—obviously.
- If you've been wet for some time, change into dry clothes, exposing as little of your skin as possible.
- Try to keep out of the wind.
- Keep your head covered (remember all that heat pouring out of it?) and wear waterproof gloves.
- Don't sit on cold surfaces—put something insulating between you and the ground.
- Eat and drink regularly to give your body the energy to generate heat.
- Keep an eye on yourself, and your friends if you're travelling in a group.

TREATING HYPOTHERMIA

If you're properly prepared, mild hypothermia can be treated quite effectively, even in the field, although you should always check in with your doctor when you get back to civilization. The key to treating hypothermia is not to warm the body externally, but to reduce any further heat loss, because a mildly hypothermic person can still generate more heat internally than can be applied safely using external sources. When you're on the track, follow these steps:

- Get the person out of the cold.
- Replace wet clothing with dry, trying not to make them any colder during the process.
- Get them out of the wind—either using a natural windbreak or by setting up a tent, tarp, or other kind of shelter.
- If they can stand, try to get them to exercise gently, to generate heat.
- If they're unable to stand, get them into a sleeping bag.

- Put a space blanket or bivy sack round the bag.
- Keep them insulated from the cold ground by laying them on a mat.
- Make sure their head is covered.
- Give them food (something like an energy bar, which releases calories quickly) and water. Warm, sweet drinks will also help.
- Don't massage or rub their skin.
- Don't warm them with external heat (such as a fire), because this may drive cold blood toward the heart and lungs and can actually lower their body temperature.
- Don't give them alcohol.

Severe hypothermia is life-threatening and cannot be adequately treated outdoors. Follow the steps outlined above and send for help. A severely hypothermic person is in great danger from heart failure and should not be moved unless there really is no alternative.

Getting Ready

Getting Going

Getting Stuck

Getting Lost

Getting Hurt

Getting Shelter

Getting Warm

Getting Food

Getting Wet

Getting Help

Dehydration

Maybe it's because most of us don't drink enough water on a day-to-day basis anyway, but dehydration is one of the most common problems experienced by hikers. People tend to think that drinking soft drinks or caffeine-enriched "energy" drinks—or even coffee—somehow counts towards their daily intake of water. It doesn't. Most of these drinks are diuretics and actually increase the speed at which your body loses fluids. So when you drink, make sure it's water.

Watch for headaches

WHAT IS DEHYDRATION?

Your body is made up mostly of water (it actually accounts for about 70 percent of your body weight) and so it needs water to survive and prosper. At the most basic level, this means your body can't cool itself down when the temperature rises and can't generate enough heat when it falls. The short and not-so-sweet of it is that without an adequate supply of water, the body's systems will gradually shut down.

WHAT CAUSES IT?

A lack of water in your body from perspiration, respiration from vigorous exercise, skin drying out in the hot sun— you'll even lose moisture from your lungs in very dry climates. Simply put, you're losing more water than you're taking in.

WHAT ARE THE EARLY SYMPTOMS?

Thirst, headaches, dry mouth, dark urine, irritability and tiredness; this can lead to breathing difficulties, chest pain, blurred vision and ringing in the ears.

WHAT ARE THE STAGES?

• With a fluid loss of up to 5 percent

you'll start to feel uncomfortable, thirsty, irritable and impatient. You may also have a flushed appearance and feel either sick or sleepy. And, of course, you'll feel thirsty.

• With a loss of up to 10 percent, you'll find it harder to breathe, your mouth will be very dry, you may have a headache, feel dizzy and be almost unable to walk; there's also likely to be a nasty ringing in your ears.

• If fluid loss rises above 10 percent, you're in big trouble—you're likely to become delirious, suffer poor vision, and be unable to understand what's happening. You need to be taken to a medical facility as soon as possible.

Cold in summer, hot in winter

In the summer months, you should drink water, as cold as you can get it. Cold water is absorbed more quickly into the body. In winter, hot drinks are important because they cheer the spirits and your body absorbs them without using too much energy.

HOW MUCH WATER SHOULD YOU BE DRINKING?

Take a good long drink before you start. After that, the easiest way to stay hydrated is to drink small amounts often. You should never wait until you're actually thirsty before taking a drink. While you're on the track, aim to drink between 3 and 4 litres (6–8pints) of water a day—about a cup every half hour. As a rough rule of thumb, if your urine runs clear, then you're drinking enough water. Remember, too, that you may need to replenish the salt that you're losing through sweat, so have something to eat as well. Some hikers are in favour of using salt tablets, but the concentrations are high and may upset your stomach.

Ration thirst, not water—drink small amounts often
➤

- Take regular drinking stops.
- One of the ways to make drinking on the go easier is to buy a hands-free hydration system—essentially a flat bottle that fits inside your backpack and has a tube coming out of it that threads down one of the shoulder straps. When you're thirsty, you just suck on the tube.
- Don't forget to fill up your water bottle whenever you can—that way you'll never be tempted to ration your supply and risk becoming dehydrated.
- Remember that if you're snacking on dried fruit (a popular hiking standby) then your body will need to rehydrate the fruit so that it can be digested, so instead of providing more fluid, this healthy snack is actually taking it away from you.
- Is it dangerous? Mild dehydration isn't dangerous at all, and drinking more water solves the problem quite quickly. Severe dehydration can put the body into shock, which is very serious. In the most extreme cases, you can die.

Replacing lost salts

Under normal conditions, if you're eating and drinking properly, you shouldn't need anything else to stay hydrated. However, if it's extremely hot or the trail is a demanding one, you may benefit from using one of the commercial hydration formulas that come as a powder and can be mixed with water. Designed for people involved in sports, they are good at restoring the important salts (specifically sodium, chloride, potassium, calcium and magnesium) that the body can lose during prolonged exercise. They're flavoured, so they also make a welcome change from water.

Getting Ready

Getting Going

Getting Stuck

Getting Lost

Getting Hurt

Getting Shelter

Getting Warm

Getting Food

Getting Wet

Getting Help

Adult CPR

Cardiopulmonary Resuscitation—or CPR—is a technique used on someone when either they are not breathing or they have no pulse. In an urban environment, we may associate this with old age or heart disease, but on the trail it can happen as the result of getting dunked in freezing cold water, being struck by lightning, or experiencing any kind of serious trauma. CPR combines mouth-to-mouth "rescue" breathing with chest compression in an attempt to restore the heart to its normal rhythm and get the victim breathing on their own again.

Tilt the head back to open the airway. Pinch the nose, and breathe into their mouth so the chest rises.

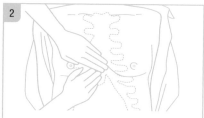

Find the part of the chest where the rib cage joins the breast bone. Put the heel of one hand in the centre between the nipples.

- First of all, some people are concerned that bad CPR technique may actually do more harm than good. Don't worry—if someone really needs CPR then they're in such bad shape that you can only make things better.
- Clear their airway by tilting their head back and gently lifting the chin. They're in the right position if their teeth are nearly together.
- Check for breathing by placing your ear near to the person's mouth, where you can either hear or feel their breath. Check to see if the chest is rising and falling.
- If they're not breathing, place your CPR mask or shield over their mouth, pinch their nose, take a deep breath, and then give two rescue breaths by breathing into their mouth so that their chest rises.
- You'll need to start chest compressions.
- Find the part of the chest where the rib cage joins the breast bone,

and put the heel of one hand in the centre between the nipples.
- Put your other hand on top and lace the fingers together. Keep your fingers off the chest and your arms straight.
- Press down about 2.5–5cm (1½–2inches) and release. You'll need to do this about 100 times a minute.
- Try to equalize the rhythm of push-and-release rather than snatching at it.
- After 30 compressions, stop and breathe into their mouth twice, then resume the compressions.
- There's no need to stop and check for a pulse, but if you notice that the person moves, coughs or otherwise show signs of like, stop CPR to see if they're breathing properly. If you believe they are, then place them in the "recovery" position.

How to take a pulse

You can take a person's pulse in two places—at the bottom of the thumb on the inside of the wrist, or just under their lower jaw bone between the big neck muscle and the windpipe. Locate the pulse with your first and second fingers and count it for 10 seconds. (Don't waste time by checking for a full minute.) A "normal" adult pulse is anything between 60 and 100 beats per minute.

3

Place the palm of one hand on top of the back of the other, lace your fingers, and keep your arms straight.

4

Push down about 2.5–5cm and release at a rate of about 100 times a minute, stopping every 30 compressions to give two breaths.

- Kneel beside them, straighten their legs and put their arms out so they look like a "T". Lift the near leg at the knee until it's bent at a right angle and place the arm nearest you across their chest. Roll them away from you, onto their side.

This keeps the airway open and prevents them from rolling over onto their face.
- Cover with a sleeping bag or something else to keep them warm.

The Heimlich maneuver

If someone is choking and can't cough the obstruction out, you may have to help them. Stand behind them and wrap your arms round their waist. Make a fist with one hand and nestle the thumb side against their upper abdomen above the navel but under the rib cage. Grab your fist in your other hand and thrust inward and upward quickly. It's important that you don't compress the rib cage—your hands need to be below it. Keep going until the object comes out. Don't hit them on the back.

You can use this maneuver successfully on yourself, but it's easier if you can find a fixed object at the right height that lets you lean your upper abdomen against it—like a tree stump or even a rock.

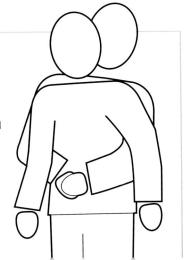

Getting Ready

Getting Going

Getting Stuck

Getting Lost

Getting Hurt

Getting Shelter

Getting Warm

Getting Food

Getting Wet

Getting Help

Fractures and Breaks

A broken bone on the trail is a big, big problem. If it's a foot, leg or lower body injury, you won't be able to walk out; and even if it's not, you may be in too much distress to move far. Every broken bone is different—isn't nature a wonderful thing?—but there are a number of basic fracture types, and it may be useful if you can recognize them. You'll find the most common ones illustrated and described here.

Types of fracture

▲ *Oblique*

▲ *Comminuted*

▲ *Spiral*

▲ *Compound*

Hairline
A tiny crack that may not show up even on an X-ray.
Oblique
The break runs at an angle to the bone.
Transverse
The break runs straight across the bone.
Greenstick
The bone bends, twists or compacts, but doesn't actually break.

Comminuted
Multiple, smaller breaks in the same bone.
Spiral
The break occurs around the bone's axis.
Compound or displaced fracture
The ends of the bone are no longer touching, and in some cases one of the pieces may break through the skin.

If you think you or someone in your party has broken a bone:

- If the person is unconscious but breathing, take advantage of this by trying to locate and immobilize the fracture.
- If the person is bleeding heavily, go to page 80, then come back here.
- If they're not breathing, go to page 76, then come back here.
- Suspect a broken bone if the person finds moving the limb difficult or experiences pain when they try, or if it is bruised and swollen or looks shortened or deformed.
- You may even—prepare to wince—hear it crack as they fall.

In the wild, all you can really do with a fracture is immobilize it as well as you can. A splint is best for this, and there should

Shock

People go into shock when the body is unable to circulate the blood properly, which in turn reduces the supply of oxygen to the vital organs. Blood loss, trauma, dehydration and allergic reactions may all cause someone to go into shock. The key is to try to restore normal circulation, so lay them down, lower their head (or raise their feet), keep them still, and cover them lightly, but don't make them too warm. Don't give them anything to eat or drink. Shock may take some time to pass, so don't be in a hurry to move on.

be one in your medical kit. If you didn't bring one or if it's unsuitable, you'll have to improvise with whatever is at hand.

- A splint itself is in three parts: the stiff part that helps keep the limb straight, the soft part that goes between this and the limb, and something to bind it to the limb.
- Straight pieces of wood or bark make good splints, and so do trekking poles; even rolled-up newspaper may be rigid enough to provide support.
- If you can't find anything to make a splint, try using a part of the body. For example, two fingers, or even two legs, can be strapped together for protection if necessary.
- You need to pad the area around the fracture to protect it from further damage. Sleeping bags, stuff sacks and fleeces all make good padding.
- Secure the frame and padding together with rope, bungee cords or strong tape.
- The splint needs to be secure to prevent further damage to the wound, but it should not be too tight, as it could impede circulation and cause more problems.
- If you suspect a broken bone, make sure the splint includes the joints above and below it.
- If you suspect that the break is near a joint, make sure the splint extends to the bones above and below the joint.

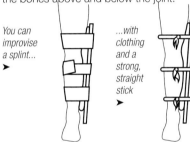

You can improvise a splint... ➤

...with clothing and a strong, straight stick ➤

Carry out

If someone in your party breaks a bone and is unable to walk out on their own, you should wait for help. If, for a specific reason, you really have to get them out, try one of these two methods. If the injured person can sit up, two able-bodied people can carry them by this first method. Both people hold out their hands, palms down. The first person grips their left wrist with their right hand. With their left hand, they grip the right wrist of the second person, who grips their own left wrist with their right hand and then, with their left hand, grips the right wrist of the first person. This forms a small hand "platform" that the injured party can sit on. Alternatively, if you can find two long poles, you can make a crude stretcher by threading one through the right sleeves of two jackets and the other through the left sleeves. Secure the jackets to the poles using tape. Bear in mind that you should not move a seriously injured person unless you absolutely have to.

An improvised stretcher like this should only be used in an emergency ➤

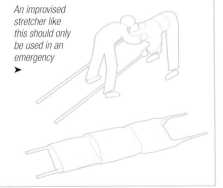

Getting Ready

Getting Going

Getting Stuck

Getting Lost

Getting Hurt

Getting Shelter

Getting Warm

Getting Food

Getting Wet

Getting Help

Bleeding

Small cuts are easy enough to deal with, but more serious lacerations are not. Your body contains about 5 litres (9 pints) of blood and can lose about 500ml (1 pint) of blood without putting your life in danger, but serious blood loss can be fatal. There are three kinds of bleeding that you can see, and one you cannot.

Types of bleeding

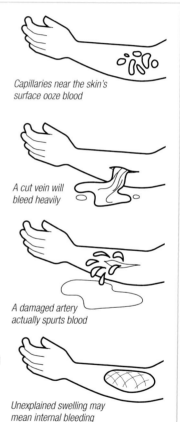

Oozing
This occurs when the capillaries are damaged, and it is associated with simple cuts and grazes. The capillaries are the tiniest blood vessels, and they ooze dark red blood.

Capillaries near the skin's surface ooze blood

Flowing
Expect this sort of bleeding from a vein when you've cut yourself with a knife. It may look bad, but can usually be dealt with by direct pressure on the wound itself. Veins carry blood back to the heart, and flowing blood is dark red.

A cut vein will bleed heavily

Spurting
On the face of it, this is the scariest kind, and it occurs when an artery has been damaged. Apply direct pressure and use pressure points (see next page) if necessary. Arteries carry blood from the heart, and spurting blood is bright red.

Internal
This is actually the scariest kind of bleeding, because you can't really see what's going on if the skin isn't broken. Look for signs of blood from the mouth, nose or ears, and for any otherwise unexplained swelling or bruising. Internal bleeding is always serious, and there's little you can do on the track aside from getting the person to lie down and raise their legs off the ground. You should then treat them as you would for shock (see page 78) and get help.

A damaged artery actually spurts blood

Unexplained swelling may mean internal bleeding

STAYING CALM

There's nothing quite like the sight of blood to bring home the seriousness of a situation and crank up the stress levels. However, many wounds are less serious than they look, and it's important to stay calm when you're trying to look after yourself or someone else. It's no good panicking at the first sight of blood, whether it's yours or someone else's.

How to stop bleeding

Elevation

This simply means raising the injured part above the level of the heart so that gravity can help reduce blood pressure and slow down the flow of blood.

Direct pressure

This is pretty much what it sounds like. Using a bandage or piece of gauze from your medical kit, press directly onto the wound. This absorbs the blood, slows down the bleeding, and allows it to form a clot. It's important not to keep checking to see if the blood's stopped flowing—5 to 15 minutes of pressure should do the trick. Even if blood soaks the bandage, don't remove it, because you'll stop the clotting process. Instead, add an extra layer on top.

Tourniquets

Despite what you see in films, tourniquets are dangerous and should only be used if you know what you are doing, or as a last resort. That is because, for a tourniquet to work, it has to be tight enough to close off the blood supply. When you do that, the part of your body that is not getting any blood starts to—literally—die. If you have to use a tourniquet, loosen it every ten minutes to see whether the bleeding has stopped. You can improvise a tourniquet with a bandanna and a stick. Wrap the bandanna round the limb and tie a single over-and-under knot. Hold the stick across the knot and tie another knot on top to hold it in position. You can then twist the stick to tighten the bandanna round the limb.

Pressure points

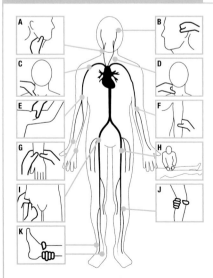

Even though direct pressure can stop arterial bleeding, you may need to use the body's own pressure points—those places where you can find, and then press, the various arteries that carry blood from the heart to the rest of the body. Locate the appropriate pressure point (see illustration) and press hard until you feel bone. The key pressure points around the body are:

A Face (below eyes)
B Temple or scalp
C Shoulder or upper arm
D Neck
E Lower part of upper arm and elbow
F Lower arm
G Hand
H Thigh
I Thigh
J Lower leg
K Foot

Getting
Ready

Getting
Going

Getting
Stuck

Getting
Lost

Getting
Hurt

Getting
Shelter

Getting
Warm

Getting
Food

Getting
Wet

Getting
Help

More Serious Wounds

Once you've stopped the bleeding, you must protect the wound from further damage and from infection. Although some people still believe that letting the air get to a wound will allow it to it heal more quickly, the best way to look after a wound of any description is in fact to dress it.

HOW TO DRESS A WOUND

- Make sure your hands are as clean as you can get them. Do this before you reach for your medical kit.
- Clean the wound with water that's been sterilized with your iodine tablets, following the instructions that came with them. If you don't have a squeezable plastic bottle, fill a plastic bag, make a small hole in it, and use that to sluice out the wound—you need a bit of pressure to do a good job.
- Any remaining debris in the wound can be picked out carefully with tweezers sterilized in the iodine-and-water solution.
- The dressing needs to be bigger than the wound by about 1cm (half an inch) all round.

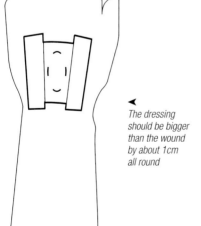

◄
The dressing should be bigger than the wound by about 1cm all round

- When the wound is clean, put some antibiotic or antimicrobial cream on the dressing itself—not on the wound.
- Cover the wound and secure each side with strips of tape. You can use clear surgical tape that's designed for this, or even duct tape if you don't have anything else (this hurts more when you remove it!).
- Keep it dry, and check—and change if necessary—the dressing every day. When you get back, check in with your medical practitioner.

INFECTED WOUNDS

If you're checking the wound every day—as you should—it's usually pretty obvious if it becomes infected. Swelling, redness, weeping or even pus are all indicators that the wound is not healing as it should. If the person feels more uncomfortable than you think they should, given the apparent state of their injury, take their temperature— anything over 38°C (100°F) could indicate an infection. Treating an infected wound on the track is hard, ugly work.

- Boil some water and sterilize it with iodine, and then leave it to cool.
- Undress the wound and, using water as hot as the person can stand, soak it for about ten minutes.
- Use sterilized tweezers to gently pick at the edge of the wound to open it and drain the pus.
- Sluice the wound again with sterilized water and then dry with gauze. Reapply the dressing as described above.

Slings

If you need to, you can make a sling from your roll of bandages to immobilize a broken or otherwise injured arm, keeping it safe and steady until the injured person can get proper medical attention. There are three common sling types.

Types of slings

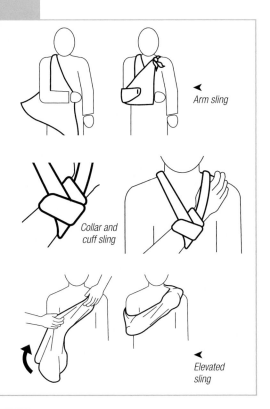

Arm sling
For injuries to the forearm, position the triangle bandage as shown here. Lift the bottom corner and tie off, and then secure at the elbow with a pin.

Arm sling

Collar and cuff sling
For injuries to the upper arm, fold the triangle bandage in half, so the apex touches the base, then fold it in half again so it's shaped like a long strip. Make a clove hitch, as shown here, and tie off around the neck.

Collar and cuff sling

Elevated sling
For injuries to the shoulder, point the hand and arm towards the uninjured shoulder. Put the triangle bandage over the arm with the apex at the elbow and one corner over the "good" shoulder. Tuck the bandage under the elbow and bring the other corner around the back. Tie off at the neck. If necessary, secure at the elbow with a pin.

Elevated sling

Improvising a sling

If you haven't got a large triangle bandage to make a sling, you can improvise using stuff that you're carrying, wearing or using around your camp, such as:

- A belt, rope or bandanna—just remember to add padding where it wraps around the limb, so that the injured person stays as comfortable as possible.

- You may be able to secure an injured arm to the person's chest with safety/blanket pins (through the material, obviously!).
- If it's still possible to move the arm, take it out of the shirt sleeve and rebutton the shirt. Then poke the arm through the front of the shirt in the gap between two buttons. This will offer some stability.

Getting Ready

Getting Going

Getting Stuck

Getting Lost

Getting Hurt

Getting Shelter

Getting Warm

Getting Food

Getting Wet

Getting Help

Animals

One of the joys of spending time outdoors comes from sharing it with the animals that live there. Most of the time, they'll see you long before you see them and they'll simply fade into the background but, from time to time, hikers do stumble on larger animals, and it's important to understand how to deal with them.

HOW TO KEEP ANIMALS OUT OF YOUR CAMP

Check the ground to make sure you're not camping where there are signs of recent animal activity. Pay particular attention to anything that might be a trail.

- Keep your camp clean. Animals have much more sensitive noses than you do and are attracted by any strong smell. Many will even eat scented soap if given the chance.
- Cook and eat well away from your tent, so that animals don't start sniffing around when you're asleep.
- Think twice about preparing foods that have a strong smell— it's those noses again.
- Don't keep food in your tent.

- Store food in a canister that's been designed for field use (your outdoor store can advise you on this). Originally designed to keep bears out, good canisters get a visual test, a drop test, and a zoo test, in which they're filled with food, smeared with goodies and left with a bear!
- If your campsite provides a food storage locker, make sure you use it.
- Hang food from a tree in a bag. The bag should be at least 13ft (4m) off the ground and 10ft (3m) away from the trunk, or something large like a bear will get it. Even if you do all you can, a determined bear may still snag your food. The illustration below shows a

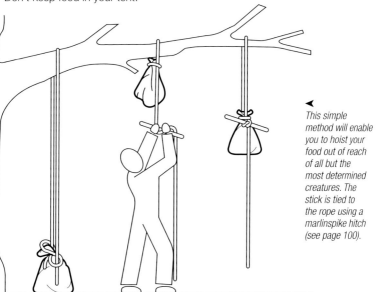

◄
This simple method will enable you to hoist your food out of reach of all but the most determined creatures. The stick is tied to the rope using a marlinspike hitch (see page 100).

simple and ingenious way to hang provisions. Simply tie your food bag to the end of a rope and create a loop in the rope. Throw the rope over a bough and pass the end of the rope through the loop. Raise the bag up to the bough and tie a stick to the rope as high as you can to prevent it from passing back through the loop.

BULLS

Rarely will you come across a more unpredictable creature than a bull - unless it's the farmer who knowingly places a tonne of potentially dangerous animal in the vicinity of unsuspecting hikers. In theory bulls are only found in fields with cows, but you'll occasionally encounter one on its own. In either case, you need to be prepared. Most of the time, a bull has no more interest in charging you than you have in running away, but sometimes something will get them riled up. If that's the case:

- A bull will usually turn sideways on at first - naturalists think this is the bull's way of showing you how big and scary he is (as if we didn't know already).
- Back away slowly, all the time trying to keep directly in front of the bull.
- Unless you can get out of danger by jumping a nearby fence or climbing a tree, dont' turn and run - the

Feral cats and dogs

There's a substantial population of cats and dogs that have gone wild and scavenge for whatever food they can find. Most survive by rooting through garbage, begging for scraps, and hunting small mammals such as mice and squirrels. Feral dogs will occasionally band together in packs but, although these can be genuinely frightening, a cheery fire and some noise will usually dissuade them. If they persist, whack them on the nose with a stick or throw stones at them.

bull will easily outpace you.
- Don't lie down. This is said to work with wild horses but a bull will just trample you.
- If it charges, quickly take off your backpack or jacket and throw it to one side of the bull at the last moment - the bull will nearly always be distracted and will swerve towards the thrown object.
- Don't try running at a charging bull - they rarely back down.

Sheltering in your car

Sheltering in a car in a bushfire is a very risky strategy. To maximize your chances of survival: park the car off the road in a place with minimal vegetation, facing towards the oncoming fire front; turn on headlights and warning lights to increase visibility; close all windows and doors; shut all the air vents and turn the air conditioning off; turn the engine off; get down below the window level into the foot wells and shelter under woollen blankets; cover your mouth with a wet cloth; and drink water to reduce dehydration. Research shows that the car's petrol tank is very unlikely to explode.

Animals

Getting Ready

Getting Going

Getting Stuck

Getting Lost

Getting Hurt

Getting Shelter

Getting Warm

Getting Food

Getting Wet

Getting Help

BEARS

In the East, attacks by black bears are Although no longer widespread, the European brown bear is still found in many mainland European countries, especially Romania and the Balkans, but also in countries like Greece, Turkey, Poland and the Czech Republic. Northern Europe has an established bear population and it's as well to know what to do should you be lucky enough - or unlucky enough - to come across one.

What to look for on the trail:
- Fallen trees with lots of bark torn off, sometimes down to the core. Bears love ant pupae and larvae.
- Torn up and discarded hornet, wasp, and other nests lying on the ground.
- Bear "nests" in trees, where a bear has sat in the fork of a tree to eat, for example, acorns.
- Claw marks on trees, where bears have climbed for the nuts or catkins.
- Distinct trails that have been used repeatedly by bears.
- Horizontal bite marks and vertical claw marks on trees, signs, and telephone poles.
- Fur caught in the bark of a tree after rubbing by a bear.
- Scat and droppings—these vary in size, shape, and color, depending on what the bear's been eating. If it's berries, for example, these will be clearly visible in the scat, because bears will eat them whole.

What to do if you meet one:
- Give the bear lots of room, at the very least 100ft (30m) and preferably more like 300ft (90m).
- If you're in a group, stay together (this makes you appear like one very large animal to the bear).
- Don't stand and look at a bear for too long.
- If you're walking in a region where bears have been seen, make a lot of noise, so they know you're coming and can get out of your way.

What to do if a bear attacks

- Bear attacks are still very rare.
- Playing dead only works in films.
- Stand your ground or back off slowly.
- Make yourself as big as you can.
- Many bears pretend to charge, shying away before they reach you.
- If the bear doesn't stop, roll into a ball and protect your neck with your hands.
- If the bear still doesn't stop, fight with sticks and stones.

Make yourself look as big as you can— stand on a rock and put your pack on your head

What to do if one comes into camp:
- Make a lot of noise by banging pots together and shouting.
- If you're in a group, get everyone together.
- Make sure the bear does not feel cornered. It must be able to see a clear escape route.

OTHER ANIMALS

So, given that most of the animal kingdom is much more afraid of you than you are of it, here are a few final thoughts that may come in useful:

- Cows and horses turn their ears back when they're annoyed or alarmed - they also flick their tails from side to side. The greater the speed of the flicking, the more agitated they are. When cows and horses turn their ears forwards however, they're merely being inquisitive - or in the case of horses just probably hoping you're going to give them a nice apple.
- The Eurasian Lynx grows to about 1.3m (4ft) and the European Wildcat to less than half of that. Both are shy and very wary of humans, so if you make a bit of noise and follow your camp rules, neither is likely to bother you.
- Wild Boar have poor eyesight but good hearing and an acute sense of smell. They're most active at dawn and dusk, when they root for food. Undisturbed they're placid, social creatures but they can be very aggressive when cornered.
- Swans are highly territorial and will fight to protect their young. It's all too easy to take a parent by surprise as nests are not always obvious and the hen will sometimes carry young chicks concealed in the feathers on her back. Although the oft-repeated adage that a blow from a swan's wing can break a person's arm may be exaggerated, it's unwise to

Rabies

Although many small mammals can give you rabies from a bite or even a lick, it's mainly carried by foxes. Even if you get bitten, only about one in six people actually develop symptoms, and then usually not for at least three weeks. Wash the wound well with clean water, disinfect and dress it. You should seek medical help immediately and get the doctor to give you a shot for tetanus as well as rabies.

argue with anything that grows to 15kg (33lb) and can fly at 80km/h (50mph).

SNAKE BITES

If you get bitten by a snake, it's unlikely to be venomous - and even if it is, you may get what's called a 'dry bite' when no venom is actually injected. Even so, clean the wound and apply a dressing. Wrap one elastic bandage above the wound and a second below it. These should be tight enough to slow the spread of the venom but loose enough for you two get two fingers under. Avoid unnecssary movement, keep the bitten libm still (splint it if necessary) and drink water little and often. Keep the bitten limb lower than the heart and get help as soon as possible.

If you suddenly need to take shelter from the elements, there are various strategies for getting under cover quickly. However, if circumstances dictate that you have to get settled for a longer stay, you'll want to be as warm, dry and comfortable as possible. Here's how to set up house in the outdoors.

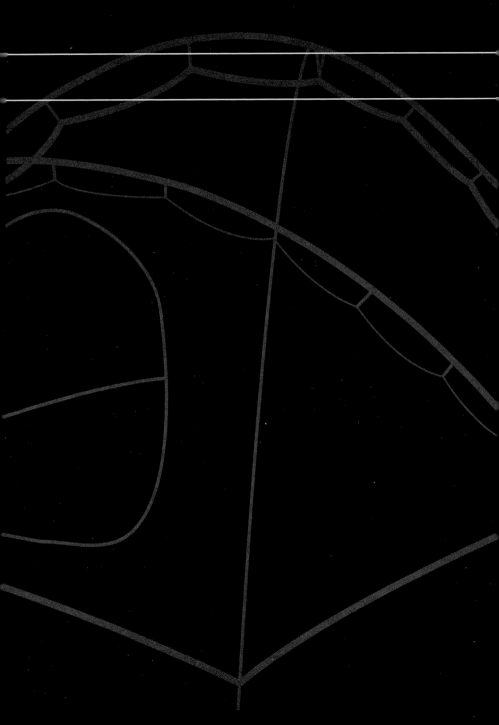

Getting Ready

Getting Going

Getting Stuck

Getting Lost

Getting Hurt

Getting Shelter

Getting Warm

Getting Food

Getting Wet

Getting Help

First Thoughts

As we've said before, anticipation is one of the keys to a successful experience on the trail, and this is never more true than when you find yourself having to cope with an unexpected night outdoors. If you have a choice, start thinking about shelter some time before you actually need it—this will widen your available choices.

Existing campsites should be used wherever possible. Consult your map to see where sites are marked either in front of or behind you. If you pass a site three hours before sundown but know there's another one a few kilometres further on, stop where you are and set up while it's still light. Well-used trails sometimes have permanent shelters.

Natural features can be used as shelter for a first night. Overhangs, spreading trees, even natural windbreaks such as rocks, can make life marginally more comfortable for one night. After that, you'll have time to think about a more permanent camp.

Investigate caves carefully and thoroughly before settling down
➤

Caves and overhangs

Although an apparently attractive choice for a ready-made permanent shelter, caves and overhangs should be approached with caution. Before bedding down for the night, consider the following:

❋ If you like the look of the cave, then the chances are that something else will—animals don't like to share.

❋ As much as possible, you need to be sure that the roof isn't going to fall in on you in the middle of the night.

❋ Inspect the roof and walls as carefully as you can with a torch. Look for structural weakness, as well as animal signs.

❋ It may sound like overkill, but before you explore the cave, tie one end of a rope around your waist and the other end to something sturdy—a tree or a boulder—at the cave mouth. That way, you can find your way back out.

❋ Light a fire at the mouth of your cave to keep you warm and to keep animals away.

Choosing a Good Campsite

If you can't find an existing campsite, you'll need to choose your own. Here are some tips on what makes a good home away from home:

- Normally you should camp out of sight of the trail, but if you're in difficulty (for example, if you're lost or a member of your group is injured) this doesn't matter—camp on the trail if you like.
- Try to make camp near water, but don't camp within 60m (200ft) of the water, whether it's a river, a pond or a lake. This helps you steer clear of animals coming down to drink, and cuts down on the number of insects you'll have to share your camp with.
- Find a level area without too many rocks and tree roots but, unless you have a specific reason for doing otherwise, don't "improve" the site by removing rocks, branches, debris and so on to make it more comfortable.
- If there's a slight rise, take advantage of it and camp there, so that any rain water flows away from your tent.
- You can shelter temporarily under a tree, but don't set up permanent camp there—if there's an electrical storm, it may act as a lightning rod. Furthermore, the drips from the tree will keep you awake long after the rain has stopped and, worst of all, a branch may fall on you while you're asleep.
- Saplings and bushes are good camp companions, because they'll help provide natural windbreaks. These will protect your shelter and will be even more appreciated when you want to light a fire (see page 112).
- Don't camp in the lee of a rock if snow is on the way. If there's a heavy snowfall and the wind is blowing, the snow may build up on the leeward side.
- Don't camp near bee or wasp nests in the trees.
- Check for signs of animal activity, particularly if you're near water—you don't want to find that you've pitched your tent on the main route to the nearest drink. Look for pawprints, paths through the bushes, and muddied areas at the waterside.
- Remember that cold air sinks and hot air rises. The valley floor may be out of the wind, but it's going to stay colder longer.

Getting Ready

Getting Going

Getting Stuck

Getting Lost

Getting Hurt

Getting Shelter

Getting Warm

Getting Food

Getting Wet

Getting Help

Setting Up Camp

Although every tent is designed differently and goes up in its own sweet way, there are certain fundamentals that apply whether you're using an old-fashioned ridge tent, a frame tent or the more modern "dome" style.

PUTTING UP A TENT

Here are some basic tips to bear in mind that will make the process as swift and easy as possible:

- Before you actually put it up, spread the tent out on the ground to make sure there's enough room to put it up—and for you to get in and out.
- If there's a prevailing wind, make sure the entrance to your tent faces away from it. Otherwise you'll end up sleeping in a wind tunnel.
- If there's a fire ring or other spot that's clearly designed for an open fire, position your tent upwind and at a reasonable distance. Sparks blown by the wind can set a tent on fire.
- Put any tent or stake bags back into your pack or somewhere else safe so you don't lose them. When you've finished putting the tent up, you'll know that everything is safe.
- If you're able to, give each member of the group a job—even small kids can be in charge of handing out the tent stakes when people need them.
- When you drive a tent stake into the ground, angle the point towards the tent at about 45 degrees (see illustrations). This will make the tent secure and stable. If you don't have a mallet, a handy rock will do the trick—and if the ground is soft enough, you can even use the sole of your boot.
- Tension the guy ropes last of all.

STRIKING A TENT

When you pack up to go home, bear the following in mind:

- Take the tension off the guy ropes before you start taking down the tent.
- Close all the zippers before you take the tent down.
- When you take a stake out, put it right into the bag so you don't lose it.
- When you get home, remember to air the tent properly (especially if it got wet at any point).

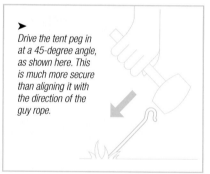

Drive the tent peg in at a 45-degree angle, as shown here. This is much more secure than aligning it with the direction of the guy rope.

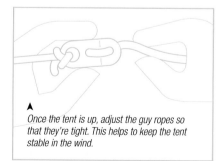

Once the tent is up, adjust the guy ropes so that they're tight. This helps to keep the tent stable in the wind.

The Poncho Shelter

The poncho is one of the most flexible items in any hiker's backpack. It folds up to almost nothing and weighs about the same, and yet, in an emergency, it can provide all the protection you need. For short bursts of bad weather, just wearing it will keep you and your pack dry, but if you need to stay somewhere for a bit longer, take your poncho and try using it to make this simple shelter.

LEAN-TO

- Pull the hood's drawstring tight, roll up the hood and use the remainder of the drawstring to secure it tightly to prevent rainwater coming in.
- Open out the poncho, take two lengths of rope and tie one onto each corner ring (or grommet) on the same side (see pages 100–103 for knots).
- Tie these ropes to nearby trees (use a round turn and two half hitches for this— see page 100) just above waist height. You want the lean-to to lean properly, so that any rainwater runs down it.
- Secure the other edge of the poncho to the ground, either by pushing sticks through the other corner grommets and pinning it to the ground or by laying rocks along the edge. This will help to prevent draughts and will make you more comfortable.

- A simple variation on this is to tie another piece of rope to the poncho's hood (making sure it stays rolled up and sealed) and tie that to a branch above. This will give you more head room.

Drip sticks

When you build a lean-to as described above, the shape encourages water to run down the surface of the poncho and into the ground. However, you may also find that water runs down the ropes tied to the trees, hits the poncho grommets and drips into your shelter. You can solve this problem by tying a stick to each piece of rope, about 2–3cm (1–1½) away from the corner grommets. Make sure the stick is pointing downwards, and drips will run off the rope, down the stick and never reach your shelter.

Getting
Ready

Getting
Going

Getting
Stuck

Getting
Lost

Getting
Hurt

Getting
Shelter

Getting
Warm

Getting
Food

Getting
Wet

Getting
Help

Tarp Camping

A tarpaulin, or tarp, is a waterproof sheet with grommets (metal-edged eyeholes), nylon webbing loops, or other means of attaching ropes and poles, positioned at several points along the edges. It's a good deal lighter than a tent, yet in the right conditions it can offer almost as much protection. The drawbacks? A tarp isn't warm enough or windproof enough to use in winter (unless you really know what you're doing) and it doesn't include a groundsheet, unless you carry a second tarp. Furthermore, unless you buy a separate bug net, there's no way of keeping out insects, and even in warm, windy conditions, tarps are full of draughts. However, they're fantastically versatile, super-light, offer plenty of room, and are safe to cook under (you should never, of course, cook in a tent). Here are some tarp configurations you may find useful:

BETWEEN TWO TREES

- The easiest way to set up a tarp is between two trees. First, tie a tight rope between the trees—the height will depend on the surrounding terrain, how much gear you've got, the size of the tarp, and how many people you're trying to fit under it.
- Use a round turn and two half hitches for the knots (see page 100).
- Drape the tarp lengthways over the top of the rope.
- For a lean-to shelter with a "front porch", stake one edge to the ground (or use rocks) and then tie two pieces of rope to the other two corners and stack them out to the ground.
- For a more standard A-frame appearance, skip the ropes and stake the two opposite edges directly to the ground.

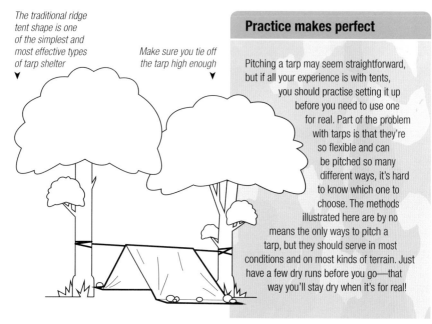

The traditional ridge tent shape is one of the simplest and most effective types of tarp shelter ▼

Make sure you tie off the tarp high enough ▼

Practice makes perfect

Pitching a tarp may seem straightforward, but if all your experience is with tents, you should practise setting it up before you need to use one for real. Part of the problem with tarps is that they're so flexible and can be pitched so many different ways, it's hard to know which one to choose. The methods illustrated here are by no means the only ways to pitch a tarp, but they should serve in most conditions and on most kinds of terrain. Just have a few dry runs before you go—that way you'll stay dry when it's for real!

In strong winds

- Drive a trekking pole or stick into the ground as firmly as possible.
- Stake one end of the tarp to the ground (or load it with rocks to make it secure).
- Attach the middle of the other end of the tarp to the top of the pole.
- Stake out the rest of the tarp.
- What you end up with looks like a conventional A-frame tent after one of the poles has been stolen.
- The end without the pole should face into the wind.
- This is also a good setup if you've only got one pole or if the ground is very firm and it's hard to get two poles in.

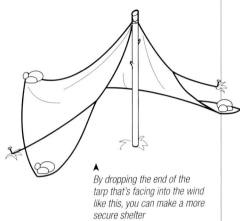

▲
By dropping the end of the tarp that's facing into the wind like this, you can make a more secure shelter

No trees?

- If you've got a trekking pole or two, you can use these instead of trees. If not, you'll need a couple of sturdy sticks. If you're in good shape and have no concerns about spending a night outside unexpectedly, then scour the ground for fallen wood and use that. If you're in trouble or in a hurry and can't find anything suitable, cut some down with your knife.
- Position your poles the length of the tarp apart and drive them into the ground as firmly as you can (sharpen the ends if necessary).

- If you just tie a rope from one pole to the other, it might work, but you can make it more secure by adding a couple of stakes and guy ropes.
- Put one stake into the ground about 50cm (18in) from one pole. Make sure it forms an imaginary line with both poles. Do the same at the other end. You've now got an imaginary straight line that goes stake, pole, pole, stake.
- Tie one end of the rope to one of the stakes, then wrap the rope around the top of the pole several times.
- Run the rope across to the other pole, wrap it around the top of that a few times, then take it down to the other stake and tie it off.
- Lay the tarp over the top of the rope between the sticks and secure the edges with stakes or rocks.

You can erect a sturdy tarp shelter even without trees
◄

Getting
Ready

Getting
Going

Getting
Stuck

Getting
Lost

Getting
Hurt

**Getting
Shelter**

Getting
Warm

Getting
Food

Getting
Wet

Getting
Help

Natural Shelters

So what if you came out with nothing? As long as you've got a decent knife and there are trees around, all is not lost. Here are a couple of simple-to-construct shelters that will keep the worst of the weather out. Just remember to keep the shelter small—it will be sturdier and able to retain the heat from your body more efficiently.

FALLEN TREE SHELTER

- If you're in an area where cutting down a tree is acceptable—and note that the practice is banned in National Parks—find a nice, bushy tree—the more foliage the better.
- Cut part-way through the trunk so that it falls over, yet remains attached to the stump.
- Otherwise, find a large fallen branch and something to prop it up on.
- Cut off the branches from the lower side of the fallen tree, so you'll have room underneath it. Next, cut the branches off the top side of the tree. Use some of these to thicken out the remaining branches to make a roof.
- Be careful when you're doing this that you don't dislodge the tree from the stump. It may not be holding on by much!

Cutting part-way through a tree trunk, like this, and then pushing it over forms a natural ridge for your shelter

▾

- Use the remaining branches to cover the floor. It's important that you put something between you and the ground, or you're going to lose a lot of your precious body heat during the night. Arranging the branches in a simple criss-cross pattern will create a surprisingly comfortable "bed".

FALLEN TREE TRUNK

- First, and most importantly, dig around with a stick to make sure there's nothing living under the tree trunk.
- Second, dig out a hollow on the side of the trunk that's away from the wind—the leeward side. The hollow needs to be deep enough so that you can put some branches down for a bed and still wriggle into it.
- Try to find some trees or bushes with thick branches and bushy leaves. Cut a few armfuls and drape these over the hollow at right angles so they're resting on the trunk.

- Pack and fill any spaces with debris such as small branches, leaves, grasses and mud. The angle of the roof will help water to run off it—a bit.
- If you've got a plastic rubbish bag, rip it open carefully and use that between the roofing branches and the debris on top to further waterproof the shelter.

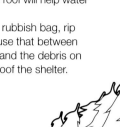

➤

Leaning a branch against a tree trunk and then piling branches on both sides of it can form a useful temporary shelter

Building a windbreak

Strong winds can sap the strength of the most upbeat camper, reducing body temperature and making everything—especially lighting a fire—more difficult. If there's simply no way to get out of the wind, you should try to build a windbreak. This can double as a reflector so that when you do get your fire going, the heat will bounce back towards you rather than disappearing into the night.

- Start by getting a couple of branches (the straighter the better) and driving them into the ground. They need to be placed about 1m (3ft) apart and should be high enough for you to sit behind them.
- For a simple windbreak, pound in two more branches in parallel positions, about 4cm (1½in) from the first two.
- Gather sticks and branches long enough to allow you to drop them down horizontally between the two pairs of sticks. Keep going until they're almost at the top.
- Tie the tops of the upright sticks together (not too tightly) to secure the windbreak.
- For a more substantial windbreak, increase the distance between the two pairs of uprights and drop in two lots of horizontal sticks with earth between them. This will be more secure, but it takes longer to make.

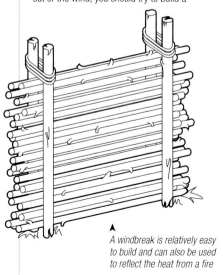

▲

A windbreak is relatively easy to build and can also be used to reflect the heat from a fire

Building a Better Shelter

Getting Ready
Getting Going
Getting Stuck
Getting Lost
Getting Hurt
Getting Shelter
Getting Warm
Getting Food
Getting Wet
Getting Help

The natural shelters we've described on the previous pages are enough to keep you out of the worst of the weather for a night—maybe even longer. The fallen tree shelter is pretty straightforward to make, and you can keep repairing and improving it day by day as necessary. However, no-one's going to want to spend longer than they have to sheltering in the lee of a log.

If you find yourself stuck outside for longer, then you may be able to take the shelter described on the previous page and adapt it to make the debris hut that's shown opposite. If you can't, then don't be afraid to start all over again. You can continue to use the temporary shelter while you construct something more permanent. The techniques described on these pages may be a touch more sophisticated but they're not beyond the reach of anyone— especially if they have a good knife, some patience and the right attitude. And they'll keep you busy while you wait for rescue.

THREE POLE TEEPEE

- You'll need to cut three poles about 3.5m (12ft) long. They should be as straight as possible but, because of the way the frame is constructed, it doesn't matter if they're a bit crooked.
- Lay them side by side about 5cm (2in) apart and bind them together (see pages 100–103 for knots).
- With the poles lashed, lift and open them to form the teepee shape and push the ends into the ground to aid stability. If the ground is hard, sharpen the ends of the poles with your knife.
- Wrap your tarp or plastic sheet around the teepee and tie it together.
- Leave enough space at the bottom where they join so you can get in and out.
- Use the grommets in your tarp or make small holes in your plastic sheet (cut thin strips of duct tape and stick

them around the edges of the holes to make them more secure—the sheeting is more likely to tear at the hole than anywhere else). If you don't have a tarp, try lowering the height of the teepee and then piling branches and shrubbery on it, like the debris hut on page 99.

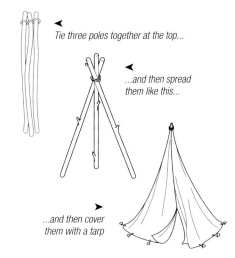

◄ Tie three poles together at the top...

◄ ...and then spread them like this...

► ...and then cover them with a tarp

HANGING TEEPEE

- If you've got enough sheeting and you're in a wooded area, you can make a teepee without poles.
- Find a tree with a horizontal branch that's sticking out at a good height.
- Make two holes in the middle of the sheet about 2–3cm (1–1½in) apart, and tape the edges of the holes.
- Pinch the sheet together so the two holes line up, and attach one end of your rope to the sheet (see pages 100–103).

- Throw the other end of the rope over the branch and then pull on it to raise the sheet to the required height.
- Tie off the other end of the rope around the tree trunk.
- Secure the edges of the sheet to the ground with stakes or rocks.
- Cut a small slit up one edge of the sheet so you can get in.

DEBRIS HUT

This is made of two components: the frame and the thatch. There are many variations for each, so let's start by looking at the three easiest types of frame to construct.

Ridge Pole

- If you're in a wooded area, cut a fairly straight pole about 2.5m (8ft) long.
- Find two trees that are about that distance apart, and wedge the pole in their forks.
- Lean smaller sticks against the ridge pole to form the roof/sides of the shelter.

Lean-to

- No trees? Lean the pole against a single tree or rock.
- Build a variation on the fallen tree shelter (see page 96).

Free-standing

- Try finding three branches about 2m (6ft) long. It doesn't matter too much if they're bent, and if you can find ones with forked ends then this will save you having to lash them together.

➤

Add smaller branches to make a thatch for your shelter. It needs to be low to retain heat, but high enough for you to be able to wriggle inside.

Thatching

Don't worry about the neatness of your frame and thatch. Instead, make sure it's as secure as possible and that the thatch is deep enough—it should be at least 30cm (1ft) thick. The more thatch you use, the better your shelter will retain heat and keep the elements out. Repairing your hut will also give you something to do while you're waiting to be rescued. Smaller dead branches leaned against the main poles make the best rafters. Leaf debris makes the best thatch (mud and moss are too heavy). Start by piling leaf debris around the bottom of the shelter, and work your way up.

- Make a teepee frame and open it out so that you'll have to duck down to get inside. The lower height makes it more secure and will keep you warmer at night.
- Add more branches as rafters, leaning against the centre, so that you have a frame on which to add thatch.

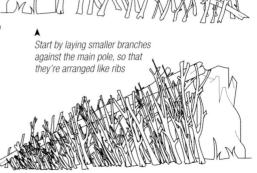

▲
Start by laying smaller branches against the main pole, so that they're arranged like ribs

Getting Ready

Getting Going

Getting Stuck

Getting Lost

Getting Hurt

Getting Shelter

Getting Warm

Getting Food

Getting Wet

Getting Help

Useful Knots

Knots aren't just for tying your shoes. Some are designed to hold tight (indeed, some grow tighter under pressure), others to slide, others to be released quickly. A good knot can get you out of a tricky situation, while a bad one will only make things worse. Here we show you the two main categories of knot, and then the two most commonly used knot in each category. These four knots are easily learned and will do just about anything you need.

KNOTS FOR TYING A ROPE TO SOMETHING ELSE

Double Overhand

A simple but clever variation on the simplest knot of all—the overhand. By adding an extra turn, you dramatically decrease the chances of slippage.

Clove Hitch

This provides a quick way to attach a line to a pole, a ring, or a tent peg. The clove hitch is also known as the boatman's knot or peg knot.

Round Turn and Two Half Hitches

One of the best ways to tie a rope to a pole or a tree, this is a strong, simple-to-tie knot that almost never jams.

Bowline

One of the most common loop knots, the bowline is sometimes called the "king of knots", because if it is tied properly, it will neither slip nor jam.

Marlinspike Hitch

Designed to hold a stick or peg temporarily, this is useful for attaching a drip stick to a guy line (see page 93).

Taut Line Hitch

This makes a good knot for tent ropes, because it will only slide one way and holds firm.

Clothesline

Dry out your clothes when you get the chance. To make a simple clothesline, tie a double length of rope between two trees. Loop the middle of the rope round the first tree and run the two halves across to the next one, twisting them together as you do. Tie the two ends around the second tree. Attach clothes to the line by opening the twists in the rope and using them instead of pegs.

ROUND TURN AND TWO HALF HITCHES

This is one of the most useful knots you can learn. It will secure any part of your tarp to a tree, and is strong enough to hold up each end of a hammock. It's quick to undo—even after a night's pressure on the knot—and rarely jams. The half hitches make this a more effective knot than the clove hitch, because they stop it from unravelling. It's also easier to tie tightly. Sailors love this knot, too, for its strength, flexibility and all-around reliability.

1
Take the rope end and wrap it once around the pole or tree. Then wrap it around again.

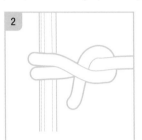

2
Take the end and fold it around and under the unused part of the rope (often called the "standing" part) and poke it behind itself to form the first half hitch.

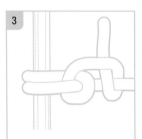

3
Repeat the previous step to form the second of the two half hitches, and then pull on both ends to tighten the knot.

BOWLINE

This is a good general-purpose knot for producing a loop at the end of a piece of rope that won't slip or tighten, but is easy to untie.

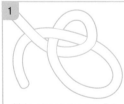

1
Make a loop in the rope. Put your thumb over the spot where the two parts cross, so that you keep the loop open, then run the end of the rope through the open loop and around the main line.

2
Bring the end of the rope back through the loop you're keeping open with your thumb. Either hold the loop or make sure it's around the object you're tying it to, and then pull the rest of the rope through, keeping tension on the main line.

3
If you want to make this more secure, tie the end off like this. Knot the end of the rope around the large loop that's been created, using a simple single overhand knot. Pull both parts of the rope to tighten and secure the knot.

Getting
Ready

Getting
Going

Getting
Stuck

Getting
Lost

Getting
Hurt

Getting
Shelter

Getting
Warm

Getting
Food

Getting
Wet

Getting
Help

Useful Knots

KNOTS FOR TYING ROPE TO ROPE

Square Knot

This is a good and simple knot that is mainly used for joining two pieces of equal-sized rope together.

Sheet Blend

This is the best knot to use if you want to tie two unequal-sized pieces of rope together.

Figure of Eight Knot

Sometimes called the love or savoy knot, this is primarily used as a stopper, but can also be doubled over to provide a loop at the end of a line.

Sheepshank

If you want to make a length of rope shorter without actually cutting it, use this knot; also good for strengthening a weak section of rope.

Fisherman's Knot

Another good knot for joining two lengths of rope together, this works best on thin cord. As the name suggests, it's a fishing knot.

Heaving Line Knot

This knot adds weight to the end of a rope so that you can throw it more easily—for example, over the bough of a tree for hanging food up.

Rope tips

- Inspect your rope for wear and tear regularly.
- Keep it out of direct sunlight when you're not using it.
- Remember that knots and acute bends can reduce the overall strength of a piece of rope by as much as 40 percent.
- If you're cutting synthetic rope, wrap the area that you're going to cut in strong tape first. Cut through the middle of the tape, and then burn the ends with a lighter or match to fuse them.
- If you use the same length of rope for a specific job every day, make sure you switch ends from time to time to even out the wear and tear.
- If you've got spare rope, don't "save it" but use it in rotation with other lengths of rope.
- If you've got soft hands, using gloves will help prevent blisters when handling rope.

SHEET BEND

 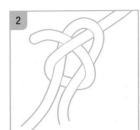 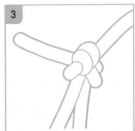

1 Make a "bite" (an open loop) at the end of the thicker piece of rope and hold it loosely in your hand. Then thread the thinner rope through and then around the bite.

2 Continue to wrap the thinner piece of rope around the bite and then feed it under itself. You should make sure that you feed through enough of the thinner rope so you can get a good grip on it.

3 Hold the long ends of both lengths of rope and pull them carefully and firmly together. If you get the tension right, you'll find that the knot won't slip open again by mistake.

FISHERMAN'S KNOT

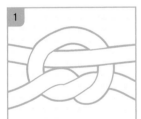  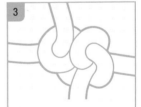

1 Place the two pieces of cord that you want to tie together so that they lie horizontally in front of you and overlap each other by about 12–13cm (5in). Tie an overhand knot in the first piece of cord (as if you were beginning to tie a shoelace) but don't tighten it—the idea is that the knot forms a loose circle around the other piece of cord.

2 Repeat this with the other piece of cord so that you now have two overhand knots, each loosely circling the other length of cord.

3 Tighten the knot carefully by pulling on the long ends of cord. This will pull the knots together and then tighten them so they can't slip.

Storing rope

For long lengths of twisted rope, hold one end between your thumb and the base of your first finger, so the end of the rope nestles in your palm. Bend your arm and then start wrapping the rope around your elbow, then take it back between your thumb and finger, then back round the elbow again, and so on.

7 GETTING WARM

Once you've built or erected your shelter, the next step is to make a fire and then to keep it going. If you're forced to make an unscheduled stop under the stars, fire is important in more ways than one: it keeps you warm, you can cook on it, the smoke keeps away the bugs, and it can attract search parties, but most of all it can help to keep your spirits up. After shelter, fire is your next best friend.

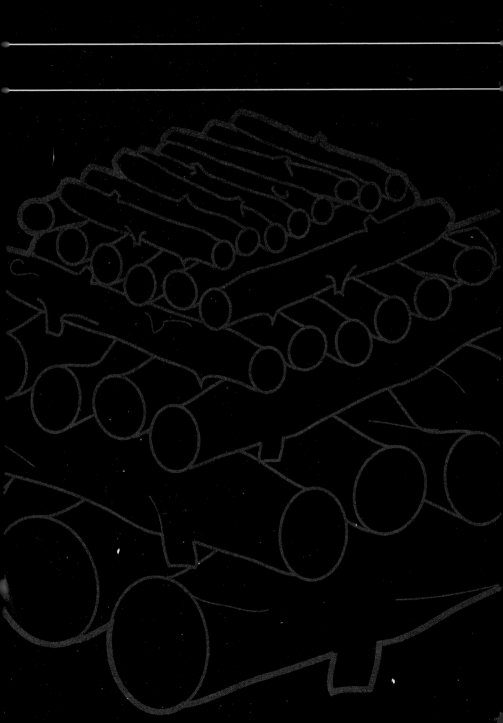

Getting Ready

Getting Going

Getting Stuck

Getting Lost

Getting Hurt

Getting Shelter

Getting Warm

Getting Food

Getting Wet

Getting Help

Where to Put the Fire

Unless it's an emergency, you can't just build a fire anywhere you like—even then, there are important safety issues that need to be considered. When you're looking for a site for your fire, bear the following factors in mind:

- You need to get it lit, so look for a natural windbreak that can work to your advantage.
- Find a flat area.
- The safest surfaces on which to build a fire are stone, sand, clay and stony or mineral ground.
- Don't build a fire too near to trees or bushes—you want to start a small fire for yourself, not a huge fire for everyone else!
- If you're in wooded terrain, try not to build the fire on rich soil with lots of organic matter around, particularly if you plan on keeping the fire going for a long time. Without realizing it, it's possible to ignite roots below the ground that can smoulder for days, or even weeks, before surfacing elsewhere and starting a serious fire.
- Clear a space for your fire by removing the top level of leaves, grass, twigs or decaying vegetation so that you're down to bare earth.
- If the wind is causing you a problem, dig a shallow trench for your fire and lay rocks on the bottom. Make sure these are completely dry and not made of flint, since such rocks may explode when overheated.
- If the ground is soaking wet, you can make a platform for the fire with green logs covered with stones.

- Think about the relationship between your fire and your shelter. It needs to be close enough to keep you warm without setting fire to the shelter, and it should be sited so that the smoke doesn't blow your way and keep you awake.

Keep it going

In order to keep a fire burning you need three things: heat, fuel, and oxygen. As soon as one of those disappears, your fire will go out. This is bad news—it's easier to keep a fire burning overnight while you go to sleep than it is to start it again in the morning. A layer of dry, green logs laid gently over the embers should keep them smoldering away until daybreak, when you can add fuel to start the fire burning properly again.

What if I Can't Light a Fire?

In certain extreme conditions, it may not be possible to light a fire. The weather may be so severe that you either can't get one started or can't keep it alight. You may be too exhausted to gather firewood, or too injured to move very far. If that's the case, it needn't be a disaster—here are some strategies that will help to keep you going until the conditions improve.

TAKE COVER

If it's raining or snowing, you need to stay dry. Try and get under cover—under a tree, or in the lee of a rock or in a cave. If you can't and you can't rig your poncho properly or get a tarp up, then at least wrap yourself up and pull it over your head so that it protects you and as much of your gear as possible. Find something to sit on—an inflatable sleeping pad is best, but an item of clothing will do.

SLEEPING BAG

If you're able to, run on the spot for a minute or do some jumping jacks to increase your core body temperature, then take your boots off, remove any wet clothing, and replace with dry gear. Then get inside your sleeping bag. Make sure the boots stay out of the weather so they're fit to wear when you can continue. If you can find something to lean against so you're sitting up rather than lying down you'll find it easier to cover yourself, the bag and your gear with the poncho/tarp.

BUNDLE UP

Put your hat on (remember all that heat escaping through the top of your head) and add an extra layer of clothing. Grab your sleeping pad out of your pack and put it under the bag so it insulates you from the cold ground.

D-I-Y HEATING

If you've become separated from your main gear for some reason or don't have any extra clothing you can stuff the clothes you're wearing with dry leaves; strip off an undershirt, stuff it with leaves, and use it to sit on; if you've got a rubbish bag, rip a hole in the bottom for your head and two holes in the sides for arms and then wear it like a tunic—stuff it with leaves and then tuck the bottom into your pants. Most important, get yourself off that cold ground—make a bed of leaves, twigs, moss and branches—and stop all that valuable body heat being leeched away. Finally, if you've got any food, eat some. This is one of the quickest ways to generate energy and get your body temperature up.

Getting Ready

Getting Going

Getting Stuck

Getting Lost

Getting Hurt

Getting Shelter

Getting Warm

Getting Food

Getting Wet

Getting Help

What Makes a Fire?

Science tells us that a fire is made up of heat, fuel and oxygen. In order to create the right physical conditions for this to work, you'll need tinder, kindling, firewood and something to light them with. We'll tell you how to light a fire on page 112 but, for now, let's look at each of the raw materials in turn, along with any related issues that may be important.

TINDER

Are you familiar with the old saying "Keep your tinder dry"? Well, there's a reason for it—of all the materials you need to start a fire, tinder is the one that's most sensitive to moisture. Because damp tinder may be impossible to light, it's a good idea to take some with you in your backpack. You can buy artificial tinder that will burn—even when wet—for about five minutes, which should be long enough to get a fire going.

GOOD ARTIFICIAL TINDER

This includes cotton balls soaked with petroleum jelly (store them in film canisters and pull them apart before

use), cotton lint from the clothes dryer, birthday candles, wood shavings, potato chips and waxed paper.

GOOD NATURAL TINDER

This includes dry grasses and leaves, fine shavings of tree bark (even if the outside of the tree is wet, the inner bark may not be), dead twigs (brittle enough to snap), dry birds' nests, pine needles, crushed pine cones and dried moss.

KINDLING

If tinder is what starts a fire, then kindling is what gives it life. Many people make the mistake of thinking they can get a nice little tinder blaze going and then just

Fuzz sticks

If your fire isn't catching as fast you'd like, try making and adding a few fuzz sticks. These are halfway between tinder and kindling. You'll need some dry, dead standing wood and a sharp knife. Scrape the wood away from yourself with the knife as if you were whittling, but don't actually finish each cut. What you'll end up with is a piece of wood with lots of curled shavings that are still attached. By placing fuzz sticks among your tinder, you'll encourage the fire to catch more quickly.

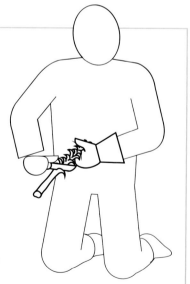

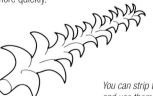

You can strip the shavings off and use them for tinder

Anything else?

Once you've got a fire going, there are plenty of things that will burn well. Pine cones are full of resin and flare up quickly, dried animal dung is good, and so are dried and empty—that's very important—wasp nests.

throw a few big pieces of wood on top to finish the job. Wood requires more heat than kindling does to catch fire, and if you try to skip this stage, your fire will fail.

It's unlikely that you'll be carrying any good artificial kindling with you, so don't worry about that. Good natural kindling is abundant anywhere there are trees and bushes. You need small dry twigs and sticks that you can snap with your fingers (growing green ones are no good); these shouldn't be more than 2–3cm (1–1½in) in diameter.

FIREWOOD

Finally, the real stuff. If kindling gives a fire life, then firewood makes it grow big and strong—strong enough to keep you warm all night and keep animals and insects at bay.

The kind of wood you can use will depend on where you are, but as a general rule, dry dead wood burns the best and the hottest. Look for wood that's caught in the living branches of trees, or otherwise off the ground, since this will be drier than dead wood on the forest floor (especially if it's been raining). The heavier a piece of dry wood is, the slower it will burn, and the hotter the fire

will be. Once you have a fire going, then green wood—and even wet wood—will burn, but it will smoke a lot. This is a bad thing if it's blowing into your shelter, but a good thing if you're trying to attract attention (see page 153). Remember that wet wood or green wood won't give out as much heat either, because they're using most of the flames' energy to dry themselves out in the first place.

If you don't have anything to cut up large pieces of dead wood, don't worry. Once the fire's going, you can just lay the end of the wood into the flames and then push the rest in, a little at a time, as it burns (see page 111).

Always gather dead wood if you can, because it will burn more easily
➤

Getting Ready

Getting Going

Getting Stuck

Getting Lost

Getting Hurt

Getting Shelter

Getting Warm

Getting Food

Getting Wet

Getting Help

Types of Fire

Lighting a fire successfully is a process. You first make the fire (or the spark) to light the tinder. The tinder must catch, and you then have to feed it with the kindling. When the kindling is alight, you can start to add the firewood. Some people prefer to build the fire on a flat surface, adding to it as they go, but the following fire types can all be used successfully in a wide range of different situations.

TEEPEE

It's a good shape for a shelter and it's also a very good shape for a fire.

- Screw the first twig of kindling into the ground, so it stands straight up on its own.
- Loosely arrange some tinder around the central stick.
- Next, build up the teepee shape, starting with thin twigs (this may take a little practice), making sure you leave a gap so you can get at the tinder in the center to light it.
- Have a store of slightly thicker twigs ready to lean on top of the thinner ones once the fire gets going.
- Either light the tinder directly or light some in your hand and poke it through the gap to catch what's already there.

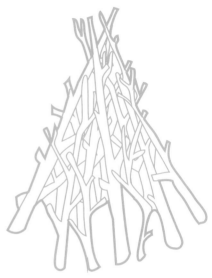

▲
Arrange your teepee fire loosely and it will catch more easily

LEAN-TO

Yes, it's another shelter shape that makes an excellent fire arrangement.

- Again, you're going to start by putting a stick into the ground, but this time it's going to be leaning at an angle of about 30 degrees.
- It needs to be a green stick, so that it burns more slowly than the kindling and will support the other sticks until the fire is really burning well.
- Once the central stick is in position, you can lean dry kindling twigs on it like ribs.
- The natural "rib cage" shape of this fire makes it easy to poke tinder under it from the open end.

▲
Use a green stick to support the kindling of your lean-to fire

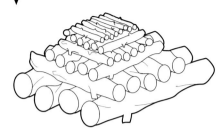

A well-built pyramid fire will burn all night
▼

▲
As the logs in a star fire burn, simply push them towards the middle with your foot

STAR FIRE

This is actually useful as a "stage two" fire—i.e. one that's already been started by another method.

- Once you've lit the fire and you're ready to add firewood, arrange your logs in the shape of a three- or four- pointed star around the central core of the fire.
- Push the logs inwards gently, one at a time, so that they catch fire.
- As they burn, feed the fire by pushing the logs in towards the centre.
- If you're careful—and you have something to cook with—you can withdraw the logs a little and rest a pot on their ends over the centre of the fire where the hot embers are.

PYRAMID FIRE

This is especially good if you want your fire to burn through the night. It is, however, harder to light in windy conditions.

- Start with two parallel logs about 20cm (8in) apart.
- Add a layer of smaller logs on top of this at right angles to the first two.
- Make another three or four layers using progressively smaller and shorter pieces, so you end up with a rough pyramid shape.
- A fire that is started on top of this will burn slowly down through the layers of wood over time.

Reflecting heat

Heat rises, but it also generally dissipates all over the place, so one of the problems with a fire is making sure that you actually get the benefits. One of the best ways to do this is to make a reflector. The simplified, single-wall version of the windbreak we described on page 97 makes a great reflector, bouncing the heat from your fire right back to you. Building a fire between one of these and a large rock will keep the heat where it can do most good.

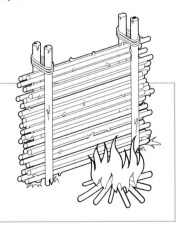

Getting Ready

Getting Going

Getting Stuck

Getting Lost

Getting Hurt

Getting Shelter

Getting Warm

Getting Food

Getting Wet

Getting Help

Lighting a Fire

OK, you've gathered your kindling and firewood, and you have plenty of spare wood under cover somewhere, just in case it rains. You've built your fire, and now you need to actually light your tinder. What's the best way to do it?

MATCHES

Since most of us are familiar with matches, they're probably still the easiest thing to use. However, unlike lighting a fire at home, you don't have the luxury of wasting half the box while you get the fire going. Special water- and windproof matches should come in a waterproof container. If they don't, use a plastic container to keep them dry; and don't forget to include a striking surface.

Safety Matches

These require a special surface to strike, and they are virtually useless on the trail, because they simply don't work if they become damp.

Strike-Anywhere Matches

These are much better, since they can be struck using any abrasive surface and retain much of their striking capability when damp. They usually have a white chemical tip at the end.

Waterproof/Windproof Matches

The ends of these are dipped in a water-resistant resin so that they'll strike in wet conditions. Most only strike on the box they come in, and that will need to be kept dry. So-called "survival" matches will burn in heavy rain and strong wind, and

> ## Drying out wet matches
>
> When any kind of match gets wet, it becomes harder to use. Only the head of a match is waterproofed, so if the stick is wet, it will burn poorly or not at all. Don't throw wet matches away. Dry them on a rock in the sun if you get the chance, or try rolling them through your hair—this sometimes works!

the "head" extends halfway down the match. They come in a waterproof container with a striking surface.

LIGHTER

Lighters make good camping companions. They're compact and can light hundreds of fires. In calm conditions, any store-bought lighter will do the trick, but for more flexibility, consider a windproof lighter. There are many different kinds available, from old-fashioned flip-tops to fancy new "turbo" lighters, designed to stay alight in the wind and the rain. No matter which you choose, make sure it's filled up and that you're carrying a spare one somewhere safe and dry.

ALTERNATIVE METHODS

Fire Piston

This consists of two parts: a hollow tube, sealed at one end, with light lubricant inside, and a plunger that fits snugly inside the hollow tube (it's important that air can't escape). At the end of the plunger there's a little hollow where you put your tinder. Put the tinder in the hollow, insert the plunger in the tube and push down hard. The compression heats the air, which ignites the tinder to form a glowing ember. An ember will last longer than a single flame.

Fire Steel

Again, this usually comes in two parts: a little rod with a handle (shaped rather like a key), and a thin, flat piece of metal the same length. The two are usually attached to a single piece of cord. Basically, you hold the handle and then scrape the thin piece of metal down the rod away from you. This generates a shower of super-hot sparks.

Lighting tinder

Sometimes this will go smoothly. Sometimes it won't. If you're using natural tinder that's even slightly damp, it will be much harder, so if you're experiencing problems, use manmade tinder if you have it. When the tinder catches, fold it around the ember and blow on it gently to encourage the fire. Hold it loosely to encourage air flow, but don't let the ember fall out. Although some people consider it wasteful, you can always have tinder already in place under your fire and then light that from a separate smaller piece. If this still doesn't work, use one of the solid fuel tablets that came with the portable stove that you should have included in your outdoor kit.

Things that burn

Good tinder
- Wood shavings (the finer the better)
- Crushed bark
- Dead, crumbled leaves
- Fluff from birds' nests
- Lint or cotton fluff
- Waxed paper
- Straw
- Dried moss and fungi

Good kindling
- Small twigs
- Cardboard
- Thin strips of wood
- Pieces of bark
- Fatwood from the stumps of felled pine trees (contains a volatile, highly flammable resin)

Good fuel
- Dead branches
- Hearts of fallen trees
- Dead standing wood
- Dry animal dung
- Dry peat

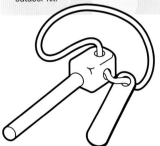

◄ *Fire steel*

► *Fire piston*

Lighting a Fire without Matches

Getting
Ready

Getting
Going

Getting
Stuck

Getting
Lost

Getting
Hurt

Getting
Shelter

**Getting
Warm**

Getting
Food

Getting
Wet

Getting
Help

Getting caught outside with no easy way to make fire is a mistake that you're unlikely to repeat, if only because lighting a fire will now take an hour or two, instead of a few minutes. Nonetheless, it's perfectly possible to generate enough heat to make tinder burn without using matches, fire steel or a lighter—you just have to know what you're doing.

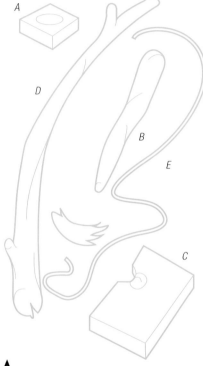

A

D

B

E

C

▲

Making a fire bow takes time, but it's a reliable alternative when you have no matches

Rubbing sticks together, for example, is a huge waste of time, because wood needs to reach about 430°C (800°F) before it begins to burn. Most people can barely make a stick smoke, let alone generate enough friction to produce fire. Similarly, using flint and steel to shower sparks over tinder is a real skill that you

may never master—from identifying the flint itself right through to striking it with the steel in the correct way. If it's sunny and you want the easy way out, turn to the next page, where we'll tell you how to use a magnifying glass. Otherwise, make life easier for yourself by spending a little time making something that looks more complicated, but that will save you time in the long run: the fire bow.

THE FIRE BOW

This is another way of producing fire by friction, only this time, you'll use some simple mechanics to make the job easier.

To make a fire bow you'll need:

- A socket made of hardwood or stone with a depression in it (A). You'll need this to exert downward pressure on the drill.
- A cylindrical piece of dry hardwood to act as a drill, about 20cm (8in) long, round at one end and flat at the other (B).
- A flat piece of dry hardwood at least twice the diameter of the drill at its widest point (C). It's often called the "hearth" and, if possible, it should be made of the same wood as the drill.
- A piece of slightly more flexible wood for the bow (D) and some cord (E).

Making the Bow

The bow needs to bend enough to keep it away from the workings of the rope and the drill and should be about three times the length of the drill. Attach the rope to both ends (if you have to cut notches, make sure the wood is not going to split) using one of the knots from pages 100–103. Make it tight, but not too tight, because you'll tighten it further when you twist it around the drill.

Shaping the Drill

Use your knife to whittle the top end to a blunt point so that it will fit comfortably into the depression on the socket (see the list of components opposite) and make the bottom into a very gentle rounded end. This allows the top to swivel nicely in the socket while the greater surface area at the bottom of the drill creates more friction.

Making the "Hearth"

Create a shallow depression in the hearth about 2cm (0.8in) away from the edge. This depression needs to be the same size as the bottom of the drill. Start it with your knife or a sharp stone, to give the drill something to bite into. Smooth it out with the drill until it turns black with the friction. Next, carve a V-shaped notch from the outside edge of the hearth to the edge of the depression you've just created. The finished shape should look like a keyhole.

Final Touches

Find a thin piece of dried bark, and place it halfway under the hearth, below the notch. Next, take the drill, making sure it's the right way up, and then twist it onto the bow line. You're now ready to start drilling.

Making Fire

This needs practice and perseverance. You need to keep the hearth steady, either by kneeling or squatting on it. You need to be able to push down on the drill really hard with the socket, and you need to be able

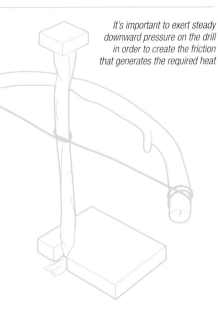

It's important to exert steady downward pressure on the drill in order to create the friction that generates the required heat

Start with a slow steady rhythm and then build up speed. Look for dark powder in the notch.

to move the bow back and forth steadily, gradually increasing the speed. Every time you stop, the wood has a chance to cool down so it will take longer if you bow too energetically and have to keep stopping.

When smoke begins to rise, don't stop. Carry on until you can see dark brown or black powder collecting around the notch. When you think there's enough (only experience will tell you this) stop drilling, carefully remove the bow and then fan the powder gently with your hand. Transfer it onto the bark with your fingernail or a twig, blow gently on it until it glows, and then tip it into the centre of your tinder. Fold the tinder around the ember so it doesn't fall out, and blow gently until it flames.

Getting Ready
Getting Going
Getting Stuck
Getting Lost
Getting Hurt
Getting Shelter
Getting Warm
Getting Food
Getting Wet
Getting Help

Other Ways to Light a Fire

Remember we said you'll never light a fire by rubbing two sticks together? Actually, we were wrong. You can—as long as you rub them together in the right way. This method is easier to set up than the fire drill, because it doesn't require any tools or rope to make it work. It takes some effort but, in experienced hands, it's an efficient way to start a fire without matches. It just may take you some time to become proficient, so be patient!

THE FIRE PLOUGH

Preparing the Plough for Use

- First, you'll need a hardwood stick that is comfortable enough to hold and work with—something about 30cm (1ft) long and about 2–3cm (1–1½in) thick. This is the piece you will be using to "plough" with.
- Second, you need to find a softwood base. This should be wide enough to remain stable as you "plough" the other stick along it, but narrow enough for you to grip with your knees—or even feet—to keep it steady.
- Next, you need to make a groove in the softwood base. If you happen to have a pocket knife with you, you can use that. Otherwise, a nice sharp stone should suffice. The groove needs to be at least the length of the hardwood stick, so you can build up a good head of steam when you are plowing. It also needs to be at least the same width. Ideally, the groove should reach right to the end, so that the glowing

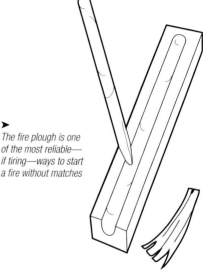

The fire plough is one of the most reliable— if tiring—ways to start a fire without matches

embers you create can be pushed off the end of the groove.
- Nearly there. The next thing you need to do is slightly sharpen the end of the stick that you'll be ploughing along the groove. This is important, because the point will help to concentrate the friction and thus heat up the wood more efficiently. It's tiring work using a fire plough and you'll need all the help you can get.
- Finally, get a thin piece of dried bark, or anything else that you can use to catch and carry the embers to your tinder, and position it under the end of the groove so you're ready to take it away the moment it catches.

Hardwood... softwood... how can I tell?

The scientific distinction between hard- and softwoods has less to do with their relative density or "hardness" and more to do with the way they reproduce. Hardwood seeds have a covering (eucalypts, brushbox); softwood seeds (pine, fir, spruce) do not. Keep this in mind when looking for the right kind of wood to make a bow or a plough.

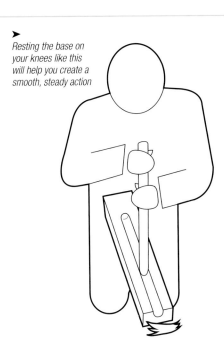

➤ *Resting the base on your knees like this will help you create a smooth, steady action*

Using a magnifying glass

On a sunny day, this is your easiest way to make fire. Simply take your magnifying glass and adjust the angle and position of the lens so that it concentrates the rays from the sun on your pile of tinder. Make sure you focus the heat on the same spot. When it starts to smoulder, gently blow on the tinder to ignite it. This requires patience, but not much effort.

USING THE PLOUGH

- Begin by pushing the stick back and forth along the groove. The temptation will be to come at the groove at a tight angle—don't. Instead, keep it fairly high—almost at right angles—until you have a good smooth groove that is easy to plough.
- Next, lower the angle of the stick to more like 45 degrees and continue ploughing. This increases the amount of contact between the stick and the wood base, thus increasing the amount of ember-creating friction.
- As the friction increases, the wood will begin to smoke and you should see black dust beginning to form in the end of the groove. You need to be careful that you don't over-plough and push this off the edge of the groove before it's ready. If you do get over-excited and

this happens, you will have to start the process all over again.
- Once again, you're looking for the dust to coalesce into a little ember that's hardy enough for you to poke over the edge onto the piece of bark and then transfer to your tinder.
- Wrap the ember in the tinder so it doesn't fall out, but leave it loose enough so everything gets plenty of air by holding it at the edges. Blow gently into the centre of the bundle, and it will start to smoke more fiercely—you can then blow a bit harder and with any luck the ember will ignite the tinder and you're in business. Don't be surprised when it bursts into flame and try hard not to drop it.

8 GETTING FOOD

If you've been looking forward to this chapter in the belief that it will teach you how to trap and skin a rabbit, so you can live off its meat and wear its fur, then you're going to be disappointed. You should only try to forage for food in the most extreme circumstances. Your number-one priority should be to find water.

Getting Ready

Getting Going

Getting Stuck

Getting Lost

Getting Hurt

Getting Shelter

Getting Warm

Getting Food

Getting Wet

Getting Help

Foraging

If you're stuck outside and you don't have any food, take comfort from this. If you're in reasonable shape, your body can go three, or even four, weeks without food. Sure, you'll be hungry as a bear, but you won't actually starve to death for quite a while.

If you're stuck outdoors without any water, it's a different story. A healthy, fit, hydrated person can go three days, maybe four, without water, but they'll be in trouble even before that. Water is literally life. As far as food goes, you should have brought something, even if you were just on a day hike, and although you may have eaten it already, your body has enough fuel to keep you going for now.

SHOULD I RATION MY FOOD?

Probably. It'll give you something to look forward to. Cooking it gives you some-thing to do, eating it will lift your spirits and skipping meals here and there won't do you any harm. If you have any, eat your perishable food first and save any dried, packet or sealed food for later. If you only have snacks, eat little and often.

SHOULD I FORAGE FOR FOOD?

Probably not. Unless you know your roots, berries and fungi, which leaves you can and can't eat, how to set a snare or trap, or how to hunt, you're better off not bothering. In fact, you're just as likely to hurt yourself—or make yourself sick—try-ing these things out if you don't know what you're doing.

SHOULD I RATION MY WATER?

No. Drink when you are thirsty. Stay hydrated. It will keep you alert so you can set up your camp properly and make any necessary preparations for your rescue.

Fishing

When it comes to foraging for food, fishing is the one strategy that's worth trying. There are reasons for this. With reasonable care, fishing is safe, and it's easy. All you need is some line and a hook. You can tie a small piece of stick to the line, several centimetres above the hook, to use as a float, and natural bait should be plentiful no matter where you are. You can eat any freshwater fish that you catch and, even if your catch doesn't taste very nice, it won't do you any harm.

Gutting a fish is easy. First, kill it with a sharp blow to the back of the head with a rock. Second, cut the head off. Third, split the belly from where the head used to be down to the fish's orifice and scoop the guts out with your knife. Make sure you get everything out. Rinse the whole thing in water, inside and out, and it's ready. You can even eat it raw!

▲
You can nearly always catch fish of some kind using a simple hand line

Fishing

As we've said, unless you know what you're doing, foraging for food in the wild is a waste of time. Bait and lure fishing, however, is a different matter.

Most fish you can catch are edible, easy to cook, and delicious to eat. Even if you don't want to eat your catch, you can still have plenty of fun. If you already know how to fish, then we're not going to pretend to teach you anything new. However, if you've never fished in your life, then read on.

Excluding fly-fishing (which is wonderful but a whole other thing), there are basically two kinds of fishing: bait fishing and lure fishing. With the first, you put some kind of tempting (to fish) morsel on a hook and wait for a fish to find it. With the second, you tie something on the end of your line that looks like a little fish or a frog or a big old bug that fish like to eat but that actually has a hook in it. Initially, an inexpensive fishing kit will serve both purposes just fine.

BAIT FISHING

You will need:
- A rod and reel.
- Some fishing line, about 2.7–3.6kg (6–8lb) test (how line strength is measured).
- A selection of floats and shot.
- A selection of hooks.
- Bait—all kinds of worms are good, but so is bread or little bits of sausage or bacon.

If you bought the line on a spool, wind it onto the reel. If the rod is in sections, put them together and then attach the reel. The line needs to follow a particular path out of the reel (this varies depending on the kind of reel you're using), so consult the instructions that came with the reel and then thread the line through the rod eyes. Next, attach the float and tie on the hook. If you drop the float into the water now, it'll float sideways. To make it sit upright in the water you need to pinch on some of the shot. Floats are usually marked in some way to let you know how much weight they need; they are also designed to slide up and down the line so you can vary the depth you're fishing at. Bait the hook, cast out, and wait for the fish to bite and pull the float under. Early morning and evening are the best times for bait fishing.

LURE FISHING

You will need:
- A rod and reel.
- Some fishing line, about 3.6–4.5kg (8–10lbs) test.
- A selection of lures.

Set the rod and line up as before and then tie on one of the lures. Cast out as far as you can. Bring the lure back in by winding the reel. Note that there are different kinds of lures—some are designed to splash enticingly along the surface, others to run deep, and others to be jerked up quickly with the rod and then allowed to sink so that they move up and down in the water. Ask at the tackle shop if you're not sure what to buy, and make sure that you purchase a fishing licence if necessary.

Getting Ready

Getting Going

Getting Stuck

Getting Lost

Getting Hurt

Getting Shelter

Getting Warm

Getting Food

Getting Wet

Getting Help

How to Find Water

If you're running low on water, you need to do something about it as soon as it's safe to do so. Don't try to find water at night, when it's foggy, or when the conditions are otherwise against you. When you're ready, here's how to go about it.

USE YOUR MAP

If you've got one, this is the easiest way. Of course, you need to know where you are (see pages 56–57), but after that, even a basic knowledge of map reading should show where the nearest water is. A topographic map has clear symbols that indicate rivers and lakes, along with wells, bores, springs and seeps. Water is always shown in blue and you should look out particularly for the dam symbol with two black parallel lines running across the dam edge—it's a road and it will certainly lead you out to civilization. Along with rivers and lakes, marshy or swampy ground will provide you with water as well. Look for any huts on the map, since people usually build near a water supply of some kind.

USE YOUR EYES

If it's safe, try to make your way to a high vantage point, so you can look at the land around you. If it's a sunny day, look for flashes in the landscape as the light reflects off the water. Even if the conditions aren't very bright, you can usually see water from some distance.

USE YOUR EARS

Sound travels a long way outdoors, and streams and rivers are noisy. Put the two together and you may be able to hear your way to water. Remember to factor in the direction of the wind as this may confuse where the sound is really coming from.

If you don't have a map and you can't see or hear water, what then? Stay calm and focused. If you follow the simple tips listed below, you'll discover there are other ways to find the water that you need but can't actually see.

- Valleys, gullies and gorges all come from somewhere. Natural formations like this are eroded over thousands of years by water, so walking down into one of these formations often leads to water.
- Dry river beds may have water below ground. Try digging.
- Look for places where the vegetation seems to grow more thickly or has a lusher appearance—it often means that water is nearby.
- If the land is very dry, any kind of vegetation means water.
- Large rocks can act as shelters for standing water and prevent it from

Why can't I find the river that's shown on the map?

It may be because it is the wrong kind of river. Seriously. There are two kinds of rivers: perennial rivers and streams, which run throughout the year; and intermittent rivers and streams, which only run when there is enough water to feed them. This might come from heavy rain, from other rivers, or from

melting snow. If there is no other obvious source of water, it may be worth following the path of an intermittent river or stream in case there is some standing water left over from the last time it was flowing. Be aware that any wells and springs that are marked on the map may also be seasonal.

Collect rainwater

Sounds obvious? Plenty of people don't do it and then wish they had. Even if you've got good stocks of water with you, until you find a nearby supply, you should think about getting water whenever the opportunity presents itself. Collecting rainwater may be lazy, but it's also effective. Although any wide-mouthed container is good (i.e. a pot is better than a bottle), a plastic sheet is best. Just take care when you're trying to pour it off into something smaller, and start by pouring it into an intermediate-sized

container before trying to get it into your water bottle. Alternatively, arrange it so that water runs down the sheet and straight into a container.

evaporating as quickly.

• The hollows in rocky ground can provide natural pools where water may gather.

HANDY TIPS

• Sycamores, alders and willows are all trees that need steady supplies of water to flourish.

• Eating snow or ice takes up a lot of energy, lowers your body temperature and actually increases dehydration, so melt it first.

• Ice produces more water for less heat than snow, so melt ice for water, not snow.

• In a very dry country, birds—or even insects—flying in a straight line are usually heading for water.

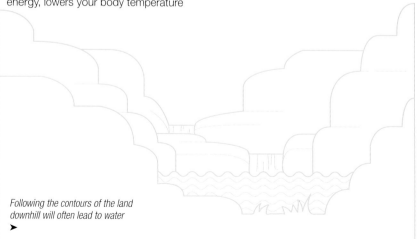

Following the contours of the land downhill will often lead to water
➤

Getting Ready

Getting Going

Getting Stuck

Getting Lost

Getting Hurt

Getting Shelter

Getting Warm

Getting Food

Getting Wet

Getting Help

Collecting Water

If you can't find water using any of the methods described on the previous pages, then it's time to take matters into your own hands. Water can be collected in all but the very harshest conditions, if you know what to do. Try these proven methods.

CONDENSATION

- The root system of a healthy tree can suck water up from far below the ground, so rather than digging for water you may never find, let the tree do the work for you.
- Find a tree with good, leafy branches that you can reach (don't use trees that exude a milky sap, which may be toxic).
- Secure a plastic bag around the branch (either by tying it or by using strong tape).
- The bag needs to hang loosely so that, as evaporation occurs on the leaves, water collects in the bottom corner.
- A few bags will supplement your supply.

SOLAR STILL

- This method usually collects significantly less water than the one described above. It works best when it's hot during the day but cold at night.
- Start by digging a hole in the ground that is about 45cm (18in) deep and 90cm (3ft) across.
- Put your cup or tin pot in the middle of the hole.
- Get a plastic sheet about one and a half times the size of the hole.
- Scrape the underside of the plastic with a stone to roughen it—this helps the flow of condensation.
- Cover the hole with the plastic sheet, pushing the middle down towards the bottom of the hole to make an upside down cone.
- Secure the edges with large stones and place a smaller stone in the middle of the sheet to ensure it dips properly in the middle.

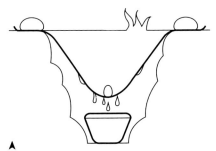

▲
As condensation collects under the plastic sheet, it runs down and then drips into the cup. Make sure the centre stone is heavy enough to produce a decent gradient.

- Water condenses on the underside of the sheet and runs down into the container.

COLLECT DEW

- The simplest method is to soak your bandanna in wet grass—the longer the better—and then squeeze it into a cup or straight into your mouth.

Carrying water

If you're fortunate enough to find a good supply of water, you don't necessarily want to keep running back and forth with your little cup every time you need some. Instead, create a makeshift bucket that will be able to carry much more. Simply take two plastic bags and put one inside the other (make sure they don't have holes). Tie the two sets of handles together and they'll make a decent bucket that will cut down on the number of trips you need to make to and from your camp.

DIG A WELL

- This is your method of last resort, as it uses a lot of energy and the results are uncertain. Remember that even if there is water where you're digging, it may be 2 or 200 metres below the surface.
- Your best bet here is to find some ground saturated by rain, or a dry creekbed with some plant growth.
- If it's a creekbed, find the nearest large plant and dig next to it.

- When you hit water, let it seep into the hole and allow the sediment to settle first before trying to decant any.
- If there's plenty of water, you can scoop it out with a cup.
- If there's not, soak a bandanna in what water there is and then wring it out into a container for purifying.

Can I drink unpurified water?

Of course, you should always purify natural or "found" water before you drink it, using one of the methods described on pages 126–127. However, if you have no form of water-purifying device and can't make a fire to boil it, what should you do?

- Nearly all natural water will have something in it that can make you sick—usually only mildly.
- If it's a choice between drinking untreated water and going seriously thirsty, you should drink the water.
- The most common water-borne parasite is called giardia lamblia, and it will give you a nasty dose of cramps, diarrohea and sickness. It's rarely life-threatening, and the symptoms

may not appear for days or even weeks after you've drunk the water. By that time, you'll have been rescued and appropriate medical treatment will solve the problem.
- Many people are immune to giardia lamblia and develop no symptoms at all.
- If you're drinking from a stream, the faster it flows and the closer you are to its source, the safer the water is to drink—usually.
- You can use your bandanna with some sand in the bottom as a primitive water filter—just pour the water through them both. It won't do much good, but it's better than nothing.
- Collecting rainwater or condensation is safer.
- Don't drink from a water source that is clearly being used by animals.

Purifying Water

Most people know someone who's been drinking untreated wilderness water for 50 years "and never had a day sick in his life". Don't pay any attention to them. Nearly all natural water sources are contaminated with something or other, and you need to take steps to remove unpleasant creatures and other potentially dangerous substances. There are various effective ways to do this and, given the choice, you should always use one of them—no matter how clean you think the water is.

Boiling

This is the most time-consuming method but it's the simplest. It's also very effective, since boiling water kills every natural organism that's in it. Get as much water as you can into your biggest pot or pan. Boiling uses a lot of energy and fuel, so you don't want to have to do it too often. Bring the water to a steady rolling boil and maintain it for about five minutes. You can now cook with it or use it in a hot drink. If you want to drink the water, pour it back and forth between two containers to aerate it again. This helps get rid of the "flat" taste.

FOR—Simple and effective against natural organisms.
AGAINST—Doesn't get rid of chemical pollutants, poisons, or metal contaminants. Requires a fire.

PURIFYING

This is essentially a water filter with an extra component (usually an iodine layer) designed to kill off any viruses in the water. Purifiers tend to be large, but you can also buy smaller bottles that work in the same way and employ a "squeeze-and-sip" system.

FOR—Full-blown protection.
AGAINST—Usually bulky and hard work. Smaller bottle-based purifiers don't hold very much water.

CHEMICAL PURIFICATION

There are three kinds of chemical compounds used to purify water: chlorine, iodine and chlorine dioxide. The first two come as tablets, the third as a liquid, but they all work the same way. You take the dirty water, add the chemical, wait a while, and then carefully pour off the clean water. It's not advisable to drink directly from the container you've used to purify the water, since one of the main drawbacks of chemical purification is that it doesn't remove foreign matter, which means that your drink is going to have stuff in it. You can get rid of most of this by filtering through a piece of cloth, such as a bandanna. General guidelines are given below, and you should always follow carefully the instructions that come with your chosen tablets.

Getting Ready
Getting Going
Getting Stuck
Getting Lost
Getting Hurt
Getting Shelter
Getting Warm
Getting Food
Getting Wet
Getting Help

Chlorine Tablets

One tablet should purify
1 litre (2 pints) in around 30 minutes.

Iodine Tablets

Use one tablet to 1 litre (2 pints)
of water, and let it stand for 15
minutes. If the water is milky or
very cold, double the time you
let it stand.

Chlorine Dioxide

This comes in two small bottles.
Follow the instructions to mix the correct
amounts together, and add to the water.
Wait 15 minutes before drinking the water.
Two 28-g (1oz) bottles will treat 75 litres
(20 gallons) of water.

FOR—Easy to use and lightweight.
AGAINST—Won't remove organic matter
(i.e. sediment), and the water usually
tastes odd unless you treat it further with
either a neutralizing tablet or some kind
of flavouring.

*Chemical purifying
tablets are easy to use
and effective—and
they don't take up
much space*
◄

*Although bulky, water
filters work well*
◄

This is basically a pump that pushes the
natural water that you've collected through
a filter and into a second container. You have
to do the pushing (or more properly, the
pumping), and it's hard work; manufacturers'
estimates that you can pump 750ml
(1½ pints) in a minute aren't necessarily
realistic. Even a new water filter is quite bulky
and heavy. You'll need to spend time learning
how to operate it and be rigorous about
maintaining it, taking particular care that
the filter itself doesn't get clogged up.
When you buy the filter, check to see what
it claims to be effective against. The
minimum you are looking for is protection
against giardia lamblia and general bacteria;
some of the newer models also list
cryptosporidiosis, a parasite that produces
similar symptoms to giardia.

FOR—Effective when kept clean
and used properly.
AGAINST—Bulky and hard work.
Won't remove viruses.

GETTING WET

So far we've concentrated on ways to have fun
and stay safe on dry land, but increasingly people
are taking to the water in search of more nautically
related R&R. This chapter gives you a snapshot of
what's important—from radios and vessel safety
checks to capsizing and running aground—and then
explains how to handle it.

Remember that knowing your equipment and
running those safety checks before you leave shore
will prevent almost all of the problems that follow.

Getting
Ready

Getting
Going

Getting
Stuck

Getting
Lost

Getting
Hurt

Getting
Shelter

Getting
Warm

Getting
Food

**Getting
Wet**

Getting
Help

First Thoughts

Boating enthusiasts know that no matter how quickly they'd like to get onto the water, there are certain things that need to be done first. There are safety procedures to go through, equipment to look over and stow properly, life jackets and fire extinguishers to check—and if you're carrying passengers, they need to be familiar with the way you run your boat. Even more than hiking or camping, boating requires planning and preparation.

THE NIGHT BEFORE

You boat needs fuel and you need food and drink. Prepare them the night before with a couple of flasks for hot drinks. Alcohol is rarely forbidden on a boat but should be treated with the same caution you'd use when driving a car. Away for more than a day? Plan some menus in advance and take the food to make them with you.

FIRST THING

Exposed areas of the boat that are wet with dew should be dried down with a chamois cloth; pay special attention to windows and any brightwork. Use rain-repellent cleaner on the windows and wipe these down with a chamois as well. Check the fuel and oil levels and make sure you carry enough to top up the tanks as required. You will also need sufficient drinking water (a typical adult needs 2 litres (4 pints) of water a day).

BEFORE YOU LEAVE

Do a weather check, look at tide tables if you need to, and select charts. Then make sure you have the necesary safety equipment (see pages 132–135), stow any items that aren't secure, and check for personal flotation devices, flares and a first-aid kit. Finally, make sure the deck is clear.

UNDER WAY

Keep a log—even for an afternoon pleasure cruise—and write down your position every 20 minutes or so both as a journal of record and in case of an accident or insurance claim. Set regular watches and then be prepared for all sorts of routine jobs—plugging a leak, mending a puncture in an inflatable, changing bulbs, switching on navigation lights, recharging batteries, practising manoeuvres like tacking and jibing, checking the rigging and so on.

AT THE END OF THE DAY

Despite spending most of their time in the water, boats do not clean themselves. Hosing down the deck, general cleaning and taking care of the head (toilet) are all usually done at the end of the day. If you've got oiled teak surfaces, wash them, then use a teak cleaner, then dry them off. Run your fingers over the surfaces to see if the washdown has done the job and if you still feel salt and dirt, wash again with a mild detergent. Check ropes regularly for signs of wear and tear. Be sure to coil and hang them properly after use (see page 146).

Radio for Help

OK, even the best-prepared, most careful, conscientious sailor can run into difficulties through no fault of their own. They can be pretty serious difficulties, too, and over the next few pages we'll look at some of the biggies, including running aground, capsizing, sinking and catching fire. All of these are serious enough to be classed as emergencies, and it's important to understand what steps you can take to deal with them. Your first port of call should be your VHF (Very High Frequency) radio. Here's how to use it in an emergency.

You can use Channel 16 on your VHF radio to call for help from rescue services. Give them the name of your boat, its position, how many people are on the boat, what's happened and what assistance you need. Modern VHF radios are equipped with a distress button that you can just press, and that will send an emergency call. Always use your radio rather than a mobile phone, which will have intermittent coverage and will only be able to reach a single person. Inevitably, there is an etiquette when using the radio.

IF YOU'RE IN URGENT NEED OF ASSISTANCE, IT GOES LIKE THIS:

- You say "Pan pan" (pronounced "pon pon") three times, followed by "All stations" three times, followed by "This is [the name of your boat]" three times.
- Then you give the MMSI (Maritime Mobile Service Identity) if you have one, your position.
- Then you summarize your current situation.
- Finish each transmission with "Over".

IF YOUR LIFE IS IMMEDIATE DANGER, IT GOES LIKE THIS:

- Say "Mayday" three times, followed by "This is [the name of your boat]" three times, followed by "Mayday" and the name of your boat, once.
- Then you and your position.
- Then you summarize your present situation and give the number of people on board ship.
- Finish each transmission with "Over".

Radio channels

Along with Channel 16—the international VHF channel for maritime distress calls—you should be familiar with the other channels that are in use where you're sailing. Typically these will be assigned to specific types of communications—for example, general chatter from boat to boat or boat to shore. In fact, after establishing communications with the rescue services on channel 16, you'll almost certainly be asked to switch to another "working" channel. There are certain channels that you can only use for boat-to-boat communications—see the tabes on pages 172–173.

Getting Ready
Getting Going
Getting Stuck
Getting Lost
Getting Hurt
Getting Shelter
Getting Warm
Getting Food
Getting Wet
Getting Help

Boating Safety Equipment

For recreational boat owners, the Maritime and Coastguard Agency requires that certain items of safety equipment be on board. These requirements differ depending on the type and length of vessel and where it is being sailed, so check with the coastguard for the exact requirements. As the skipper, you are responsible for all safety measures.

What follows is a run-down of things that you'll need to carry, based on what Her Majesty's Coastguard recommends. Not all of these will apply to you; it depends on the kind of boat you use, where you take it out, and where the boat is registered (if it is registered). Still, when it comes to safety, it's best to start at the top and work down.

DISPLAY OF NUMBERS

Commercial or large vessels (usually over 5.5m long) must be registered. If your boat is registered, the registration number needs to be displayed permanently on the forward part of the boat on each side. Sailing vessels may display the registration numbers on the transom. The colour must contrast well against the background; the characters must be at least 15cm high; the letters and numbers must be in a clear font that can clearly identified.

PERSONAL FLOTATION DEVICES (PFDs)

You'll need one life jacket per person on the boat, and they must fit properly; an adult's PFD will not be suitable for a child. They must be easily accessible and immediately available for use—not still in the plastic bag they came in. Boats being usd in open (ocean) waters must carry Type 1 lifejackets—these give the highest level of bouyancy and can keep an unconscious person's head above water. Boats in enclosed waters may use Type 1, 2 or 3 jackets—the latter two types provide bouyancy but lack the ability to keep the wearer's head out of the water.

LIFEBUOYS

Lifebuoys are required on larger boats. Generally, those over 8m (26ft) long should have one, while boats over 13.7m (45ft) need two.

VISUAL DISTRESS SIGNALS

The requirement here varies depending on whether the boat is being used on coastal or enclosed waters (and, in some places, on how far from the coast you are sailing); you should certainly have at least one day and one night pyrotechnic device and maybe some alternatives; for example, a strobe light,

◄

Three different styles of life jacket

VISUAL DISTRESS SIGNALS

red hand flare—
day and night use

torch—*night use only*

arm signals
(wear bright clothing)

orange smoke signal *(hand)—*
day use only

parachute red—
day or night

signal mirror, torch or lantern. A quick and dirty way of indicating if you are in trouble is to fly your ensign upside down. In some areas, red star parachute distress rockets are required by many vessels when venturing greater than 2 nautical miles from the shore.

FIRE EXTINGUISHERS

In most jurisdictions, you'll need these if the boat has an electric start motor, gas installation or fuel stove, or where any fuel is carried. The extinguishers must be

Extinguishers

WATER	FOAM	DRY POWDER	CO$_2$	WET CHEMICAL
Wood, paper, fabrics, etc. Do not use on live electricity.	Solids and flammable liquids. Do not use on electricity.	Solids, liquids, and gases. Safe on electricity, but messy.	Electricity and flammable liquid fires. Ventilate area after use.	Cooking oils and fats.

Remember that specific extinguishers—water, foam spray, dry powder, CO$_2$, and wet chemical—are required to tackle different kinds of fire.

Boating Safety Equipment

Getting Ready

Getting Going

Getting Stuck

Getting Lost

Getting Hurt

Getting Shelter

Getting Warm

Getting Food

Getting Wet

Getting Help

easy to get at, and work properly. There are different requirements regarding the number of fire extinguishers, depending on the boat's length. There are different types of fire extinguisher, each suited to a particular type of fire. A dry powder extinguisher is a good general purpose type which will work well on most fires.

SOUND-PRODUCING DEVICES

It's a good idea to have something like a whistle, siren or horn.

FIRE BUCKET/BAILER

You may need to carry a fire bucket. This can double as a bailer if certain conditions are met—e.g. that it's secured by a lanyard and that it's sturdy enough to hold water without distorting.

NAVIGATION LIGHTS

You're expected to display navigation lights between sunset and sunrise, or during daylight hours if the conditions warrant it—for example, in fog. Check local regulations for the number of

lights needed and their location.

WASTE DISPOSAL PLACARD

In some regions, boats over 8m (26ft) must display a placard explaining what kind of dumping is prohibited, and where. Boats over 13.7m (45ft) must also display a written waste disposal plan.

MARINE SANITATION DEVICES

If you have a toilet, it must be an approved device and you must be able to seal any outlets to prevent discharge.

NAVIGATION RULES

You should also have a copy of the current rules of navigation.

OTHER EQUIPMENT

An anchor, chain and line are required on many vessels operating on coastal and enclosed waters, and a compass, marine radio and EPIRB (emergency beacon) also need to be carried on vessels operating offshore.

GENERAL BOAT CONDITION

A safe boat has a deck that's clear and hazard-free, and there should be no obvious fire hazards. The bilges should be reasonably clean, and there should

be an electric or manual bilge pumping system. The electrical system should be fused, or use circuit breakers that can be manually reset. Fuses and switches must be covered properly to protect them from spray damage, and there should be no exposed wiring at all. Batteries must be secured properly and their terminals protected to prevent dangerous arcing; all personal watercraft require a "kill-switch" mechanism. Portable fuel tanks must be free of corrosion and leaks, and made of non-breakable material, with vapour-proof caps; they must also be secured. All permanent tanks must be ventilated properly. Galley and any heating systems must be properly secured and the area clear of any and all flammable material.

of a boat and gives an opinion on its safety and value. The surveyor looks at the condition and value of a boat for the owner, prospective buyer, bank or insurance company. A marine survey is recommend for your vessel every three years or after any major modifications. A survey is also recommended for anyone in the market to buy a vessel.

RANDOM CHECKS

Another good reason to keep your vessel's safety equipment up to scratch is the prospect of random checks by local government maritime safety officials. If your vessel is found wanting, you may be fined or even have your boating licence suspended. Random safety checks regularly reveal boats that fail to meet safety and registration requirements.

WHAT'S A MARINE SURVEY?

A marine surveyor makes an inspection

When should I wear a PFD?

Some places have legislation covering this, so just check the regulations before you go. Otherwise, you should wear a PFD if there are lots of other boats about, if the weather conditions are poor, if the water conditions are uncomfortable, if you're a long way from shore, if it's dark or there is low visibility, or if you're alone on the boat. In fact, any time you feel like you should be wearing your PFD, you should put it on—it's much harder to get into one on a

rocking boat, or worse still, in the water, than in calm and unhurried conditions.

Getting Ready

Getting Going

Getting Stuck

Getting Lost

Getting Hurt

Getting Shelter

Getting Warm

Getting Food

Getting Wet

Getting Help

Running Aground

This is what happens when the bottom of your boat meets the bottom of the lake, river or sea that, moments before, you were skimming over and probably not paying very much attention to. There are various degrees of running aground, depending on the different factors involved, but two crucial components dictate how serious it is: the speed the boat is travelling at when it hits, and the physical makeup of the bottom itself. It's possible, for example, to come to the gentlest of stops on a sandbank without causing any damage at all; but then again you can whack into razor-sharp rocks and rip out half the bottom of the boat before you know what hit you.

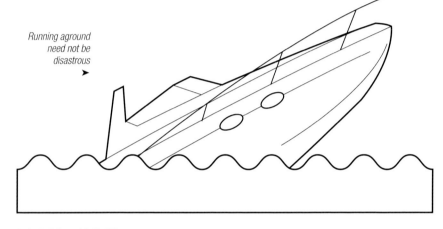

Running aground need not be disastrous ➤

HOW TO AVOID IT

Learn how to read a chart properly, so you can avoid shallow water and not get into this trouble in the first place. Understand your boat as well as you can: how deep the rudder and centreboard go (and thus how deep your draft is), how to raise them quickly if you need to, how to tell the depth of the water around you either visually or by using a depth sounder.

HOW TO DEAL WITH IT

Whatever you do, you need to be decisive and act quickly. If you're fortunate enough to have run slowly into sand and you're alert, it may be possible just to steer straight back out again. If not, get the sails down if you have them, as this will stop you being pushed further aground. Got a centreboard?—pull it up fast. Try rocking the boat to one side to reduce the draft (this is called "heeling"), and if you can, get someone to check the bilges to make sure you're not taking on water. If the rudder isn't stuck, you may be able to reverse off with your engines. To reduce your draught, try getting rid of any heavy objects by dumping them into a dinghy. Set the anchor, and either try and use it to pull yourself off, or wait and see if the tide will float you off. Although it might look like the easy way out, only take a tow as a last resort, in case the boat is damaged by being pulled off the rocks.

Capsizing

This is what happens when your boat tilts over so far that it goes onto its side and starts to ship water; in extreme circumstances, it will actually "turn turtle" and go completely upside down. Though this is potentially unpleasant and awkward, the design of modern boats makes them easier to right than ever before, and if your gear is stowed away properly, you may not even lose anything.

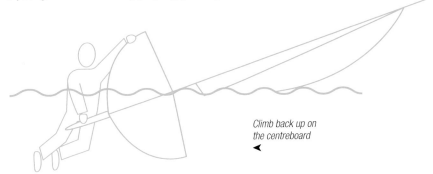

Climb back up on the centreboard
◄

The ease with which you can right a small capsized boat depends on the type of boat. A modern dinghy, for example, is designed to drain water really quickly, and sits high in the water so it's easier to get back up. A catamaran, on the other hand, is difficult or impossible to right.

HOW TO AVOID IT

Most power boats are very difficult to flip. In a sailboat, keep an eye on the wind and the sails so that your boat doesn't simply blow over, as this is the most common cause of a capsize. Watch for large waves and the wakes of large boats, as these can rock you over. If you're in a canoe or a kayak, then it's hard to capsize in flat, calm water; however, a large unexpected wave, the wake of a thoughtless boat, and human error can all result in a full capsize.

HOW TO DEAL WITH IT

If you have a sailboat with a centreboard, you've got the opportunity to climb gracefully up onto the gunwale as the boat goes over, before stepping down onto the centreboard. There you can keep everything nice and balanced while you work out what to do next. Resist the natural temptation to throw yourself onto the sail as it goes over; this is really stupid, as you'll more than likely just sink the mast. If you can't climb over elegantly, then swim around to the centreboard. Before you try and right the boat, cast off the sheets—otherwise you're likely to capsize all over again before you can get her up. Righting a canoe when you're still in it is a specialized skill beyond the scope of this book.

▲
Modern dinghies are designed so that the water drains away quickly, making them easier to right

Getting
Ready

Getting
Going

Getting
Stuck

Getting
Lost

Getting
Hurt

Getting
Shelter

Getting
Warm

Getting
Food

Getting
Wet

Getting
Help

Sinking

Should your boat sink, or be impossible to right, then you've got some important decisions to make. Actually, you've got one important decision to make: should you stay with the boat, or try and swim to shore and safety?

The answer, however, if simple: no matter how close land appears, always stay with the boat as long as it's afloat. Here's why:

- It's likely to help you to stay afloat; indeed, you may even be able to climb onto it while you wait for help.
- Assuming you got off a radio message with your position, people are going to come looking for you, and your boat is a lot easier to see bobbing in the water than you are, so stay close to it.

If your boat is upside down and drifting, still stay with it, unless it's clearly drifting into danger; if there's more than one of you, stick together.

If you're in the water, however, adopt the so-called HELP position—Heat Escape Lessening Posture—by pulling your

knees into your chest, crossing your feet, crossing your arms over your chest, and letting your personal flotation device do the work. This will help you to retain more body heat (which is vital, because even warm water will leach heat out of your body more quickly than you might think) and relax you so you can conserve energy.

The HELP (Heat Escape Lessening Posture) position ◄

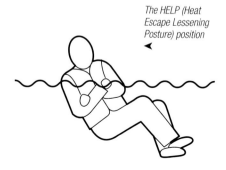

Fire Onboard

Fire on a boat can be a killer. It can cause panic and confusion, and when you add to that a collection of people in a confined space who may not be familiar with the boat or with proper fire procedures, you've got a recipe for disaster. Fortunately, it's possible to take plenty of steps to prevent fires on board.

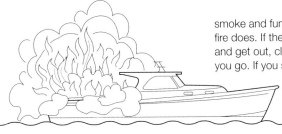

HOW TO AVOID IT

Make a fire action plan so that there's an escape route for every sleeping position. Make sure your routes are usable—that they're not blocked, they're big enough, and hatches open properly (or, if your route involves a window, that there's a readily available means to break it). Everyone needs to run through the route in their heads so that they're confident they know their steps to escape, even in the darkness and confusion of an onboard fire. Turn off appliances when not in use, and NEVER leave a lit stove unattended. If you can't live without candles, make sure they're in robust, stable containers, away from draughts and anything else that can catch fire; blow them out when you leave the cabin. Use safety matches only, and keep them away from the kids. Don't smoke in bed; better still, don't smoke at all. Clean the bilges regularly of oil residue and other flammable stuff. Install alarms that detect smoke, gas and fuel vapour.

HOW TO DEAL WITH IT

Radio for help, and get everyone into a life jacket. Use your extinguishers to put out a small fire, keeping your head low—smoke and fumes kill more people than fire does. If the fire is spreading, give up and get out, closing doors behind you as you go. If you suspect an engine-room fire, don't open the hatch to check, or the increase in oxygen may create a flash fire. If you're able to, turn off gas cylinders and anything else flammable. Don't pick up something that's on fire in order to throw it overboard—you're just likely to spread the fire. Never try and put out a deep-fryer fire with an extinguisher, because you'll just splatter burning fat everywhere; extinguish it with a fire blanket instead. Finally, get everyone off the boat and into the dinghy; remember that a fire can reignite even after you think you've put it out.

Fire extinguisher symbols

 Suitable for common materials such as paper, wood, or most other combustibles

 Flammable liquids such as gasoline, paint remover, or grease

 Electrical fires

 Combustible metals usually found in industry

Getting
Ready

Getting
Going

Getting
Stuck

Getting
Lost

Getting
Hurt

Getting
Shelter

Getting
Warm

Getting
Food

Getting
Wet

Getting
Help

Person Overboard

Falling overboard can range from an inconvenience to a genuinely life-threatening situation, depending on the circumstances and the person involved. Very few people are injured in the act of falling overboard; most problems arise because they're not wearing a personal flotation device, and/or are unable to get back into the boat.

HOW TO AVOID IT

Be aware of what's going on around you, so you can anticipate sudden movements in the boat that would otherwise catch you unawares. Practise the idea of "one hand for the boat and one hand for yourself" (i.e. never move around the boat without holding onto something). There's rarely room for horseplay on a boat, and anyone who's had a drink needs to be especially careful. It's good practice to keep decks, companionways and stairs free from obstructions. When you're standing still, bending your knees will give you better balance.

HOW TO DEAL WITH IT

Immediately shout "Man overboard" and throw a lifebuoy and line. Aim slightly upwind of the victim and throw with an underarm motion, which will give you better control and distance. Make sure you keep them in sight the whole time; if you can't, get someone else to do it—it can be very hard to find someone again in the water once you've lost sight of them. Now turn the boat in the direction in which they fell; this will move the rudder and propeller away from them.

Try to approach them by heading into the wind or the waves; this will give you more control over the boat and stop it from drifting into them. When you come alongside, use a combination of the flotation device (which they should be hanging on to) and a boathook to get them on board, keeping nice and low as you do, so they don't overbalance you and pull you in with them.

Solo sailor overboard

If you're out alone and you end up in the water, it can be really difficult to get back into the boat. Some larger boats have a platform that you can climb onto, or a ladder, but others have nothing. On a small boat you'll need to try and pull yourself up out of the water to the point at which your chest is partly in the boat, then kick your legs as if you were swimming, and then give a final heave so you kind of tip forward into the boat. But this is exhausting, and not guaranteed to work. Solo sailors should carry a personal light and a whistle.

Carbon Monoxide

This is probably the single most toxic substance you'll come across in your everyday life, and under the right conditions it's a killer—a killer that you can't see, smell or taste. That's why it's important to understand what it is, what it does, and how to avoid it.

WHAT IS IT?

It's a poisonous gas produced by the incomplete burning of carbon-based fuels—such as petrol or diesel in an engine—that's especially dangerous when it collects unnoticed.

WHAT HAPPENS?

When you breathe it in, carbon monoxide goes into the lungs and displaces the oxygen in the bloodstream. When your body doesn't get the oxygen it needs, the consequences are always serious and can result in death. Common symptoms of carbon monoxide poisoning are problems with your vision, dullness and confusion, headaches, nausea, weakness and dizziness. These symptoms are often mistaken for those of seasickness. Even a short exposure to high levels of carbon monoxide can result in death.

WHERE IS IT?

Since it's produced by the engine, it's going to be in and around there as well as in the exhaust. Serious problems can arise if the exhaust is blocked, because this can result in carbon monoxide collecting elsewhere on the boat, even in the cabin or cockpit; indeed, if there's a boat idling nearby, you should try and stay at least 6m (20ft) away from it. If there's a tailwind, or if you're running with the bow too high in the water, this may cause carbon monoxide to build up.

Easily the most dangerous area is at the stern of the boat, where carbon monoxide can collect around the swim platform; if you think about it, this is a pretty stupid place to encourage people to get in and out of the water, since the propeller is also there, just under the water and out of sight. If people are spending time in the water where an engine is leaking the gas out of the exhaust, then they're in a danger area.

WHAT CAN YOU DO ABOUT IT?

Buy carbon monoxide detectors and take advice about where to put them on your boat. Make sure they work before each trip. Shut valves on propane tanks when you leave the boat. If you suspect that someone has carbon monoxide poisoning, then move them into fresh air immediately. If you've got oxygen (this is unlikely), administer it. Get them to a medical professional as soon as you can, radioing ahead for help if you suspect their condition is serious. People with mild carbon monoxide poisoning will usually make a full recovery with no lasting after-effects—however, as many as half of those who have serious CO poisoning will suffer from long-term health problems as a result of damage to the heart.

Getting Ready
Getting Going
Getting Stuck
Getting Lost
Getting Hurt
Getting Shelter
Getting Warm
Getting Food
Getting Wet
Getting Help

Mechanical Trouble

All boats are machines. They may be as old-fashioned as a wooden canoe or as space-age as a kevlar kayak; they may be complex, like a single-person sailboat, or powered by sophisticated engines, like a modern motor yacht. But if they've got parts, they've got parts that can go wrong.

AN OUNCE OF PREVENTION...

...is worth a pound of cure, so the saying goes; so it'll be no surprise to hear that we recommend you keep your craft in fighting trim by looking after it properly. That means maintenance. Boats are just like cars in that they respond well to being looked after and kept clean; if they use stuff that needs replacing (like oil and antifreeze), then keep an eye on it and replace it in good time. No-one likes doing the boring jobs when they could be out enjoying the boat, but always remember that it's much easier to ensure your boat doesn't break down, than to fix it if it does.

The obvious thing to do is to get to know your boat, to listen to its moods and understand what's going on. If something starts behaving oddly—or just differently—make a point of investigating it by either returning to shore early or arriving early next time you want to go out. Ninety percent of the time there won't be anything wrong at all, but in the other 10 percent of cases what you discover will be enough to prevent a breakdown. Explore your boat. Find out where the pipes and cables run, check the equipment, look for leaks and anything else that shouldn't be happening, and fix it before it becomes a problem.

ENGINE FAILURE

Fifty percent of mechanical problems are engine-related, so if your boat hasn't got one, good for you. If it has, then the first thing you should do before you take it out is to check it thoroughly and regularly to make sure all is well. Maintenance checklists vary with engine type, make and installation, but typically include the following:

• Check the engine mounts for cracks or breaks, and look to see if any other fittings appear in poor condition; then check belts and hoses for the same.
• While you're there, look for leakage around the hoses and gaskets, and check to see if there's any oil in the bilge; if there is, it could be leaking from the engine.
• Check the oil level, and make sure the oil itself isn't milky, because that's one of the signs that water has got into the engine at some point.
• Look for white residue on the engine, which can indicate that it is running too hot.
• Are the spark plugs worn or burnt?

then change the fuel filters as well.

OTHER CONSIDERATIONS

Although the majority of your problems are going to be engine-related, there are plenty of other things to go wrong on a boat:

- Regularly check the sails, rigging, ropes and all the hardware on your sailboat.
- Open and close hatches—you'll be especially glad that they close properly if you hit some rough weather.
- Examine electrical connections for rust.
- When you can, do a thorough check of the hull while the boat is out of the water. Look for stress cracks, chipping, cracks in the gel coat, blisters on the hull, and any other bumps and bruises.
- Check the condition of the rudder and tiller, and the dagger board if you have one.
- Check that your boat's batteries are firmly secured and sit properly in their acid-proof containers.
- Check your fuel tanks and lines— use your nose as well as your eyes.
- If you're preparing to store your boat for the winter, drain the fuel tanks as much as possible and then refill them; make sure you add a stabilizing agent at this stage and

Your boating toolbox

Although it's possible to buy a boating toolkit, many of the tools are the same as the ones you'd buy in a decent car accessories store. The one thing the toolbox may have going for it is that it should be waterproof and float. You can fill it with an assortment of spanners, Phillips and slotted screwdrivers, a couple of hammers, needle-nose pliers, locking pliers and wire cutters— and check to see if anything needs an Allen key; if it does, pack a set with multiple sizes. Just as important, you need to carry spares for important components like hoses, belts, spark plugs and fuses; electrical and duct tape; a selection of plastic zip ties; spare water and oil.

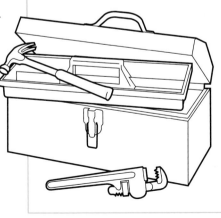

Getting Ready

Getting Going

Getting Stuck

Getting Lost

Getting Hurt

Getting Shelter

Getting Warm

Getting Food

Getting Wet

Getting Help

Celestial Navigation

Why would you want to know how to navigate by the stars when you've got a GPS and all the technology that a modern boat can offer? Partly because things can go wrong or break down, and partly because if you're any kind of sailor, you just want to know how this stuff works. And that's reason enough to find out a bit more about it.

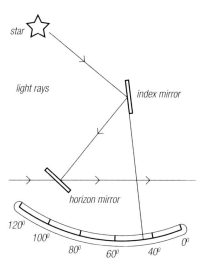

star

light rays

index mirror

horizon mirror

120°
100°
80°
60°
40°
0°

WHAT IS CELESTIAL NAVIGATION?

Basically, it's a way of using the sun and the stars to find out where you are. This has obvious advantages (there's no electrical or electronic equipment to break down) as well as disadvantages (you have to have a clear sky in order to see a celestial object in the first place). That said, in order to navigate by the stars you need three things:

- a sextant, which is a device that measures the angle of the sun or one of 56 other stars (chosen for their brightness and their distribution in the sky) above the horizon.
- a marine chronometer, which is essentially a watch that continues to

work on a ship; this may sound pretty basic, but the most accurate early timepieces typically used pendulums, which simply didn't work on a boat because of the way it rolls around.

- a current nautical almanac, which contains the positions of all the relevant celestial bodies for each second of the year.

HOW DOES IT WORK?

- You have to point the sextant at a particular celestial object; for example, the sun or a bright star. (Sextants have filters to prevent your eyes being damaged by direct sunlight.)
- Then you adjust the sextant until the object appears to be "sitting" on the horizon and note the reading on the indicator and the micrometer drum. (The sextant has mirrors and lenses that allow you to move the apparent location of the sun down to the horizon.)
- Once you've got that figure, you need to write it down quickly, because waiting only a few seconds can put you off by a nautical mile.
- Next, you check the nautical almanac, a book of tables that lists the exact position of each of those 57 celestial bodies (remember, that's the sun and 56 other particularly bright stars) at every time of day.
- You'll then have to go through a series of corrections to take into account instrument error, refraction and other unavoidable factors.
- Next, it's necessary to check through a second set of tables to confirm the name

A little history

For years, sailors used the sun and stars to go from east to west, or vice versa, along a line of latitude. This was fine up to a point, and many times they eventually bumped into one piece of land or another. However, there was no way of establishing longitude until someone invented a clock that worked properly at sea and that—used in conjunction with a nautical almanac— allowed sailors to establish their local time relative to Greenwich mean time. Since the sun moves 15 degrees an hour, it's possible to work out your longitude from that.

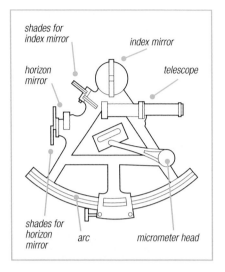

shades for index mirror

index mirror

horizon mirror

telescope

shades for horizon mirror

arc

micrometer head

of the celestial body, its vertical angle (in degrees, minutes and seconds), and when you took the measurement; this allows you to plot your position. Getting an accurate sighting with a sextant takes practice—make sure you do this on a moving boat rather than on dry land, which doesn't go up and down!

- You can't use a sextant on cloudy days, because you have to be able to see the sun and/or stars.
- The best time to use a sextant is at dawn or dusk, because then you can see both the celestial bodies and the horizon more clearly (though modern sextants have a way of creating a false horizon if you can't see the real one).
- Sextants are designed for right-handed people—that is, they are held in the right hand and the adjustments to the index arm are made with the left hand.

But I can't afford a sextant

A typical sextant is an expensive piece of equipment—even second-hand, it's likely to cost more than most people will want to spend on something that may end up only being used rarely. However, by scouring the internet we found one that was very reasonably priced. True, it's made of laminated cardboard and you have to build it yourself, but the manufacturer claims that it has an accuracy of "better than eight minutes of arc", which is certainly enough to give you a better-than-ballpark indication of where you are. It includes full instructions for building and using the sextant, as well as an almanac of the sun. And where there's one reasonably priced cardboard sextant, you can bet there are others.

Getting Ready

Getting Going

Getting Stuck

Getting Lost

Getting Hurt

Getting Shelter

Getting Warm

Getting Food

Getting Wet

Getting Help

Storing Rope

Rope that is dumped after use anywhere on the boat immediately becomes a hazard. Even worse, it starts to deteriorate—and for something seemingly so strong and solid, it deteriorates quickly. Given the key role played by rope on most boats, it's important to look after it properly.

1	2	3	4

If you are right-handed, hold the rope in your left hand and make coils with your right. Twist the rope away from you between thumb and forefinger so that the coils form circles.	Finish coiling the rope leaving a long working end. Wrap this several times around the coils to bind them together.	Make a loop with the remainder of the working end and push this through the top of the coil, above the binding.	Pull the loop over the top of the coil and down to the bound part, then pull the working end to secure it.

You should always coil a rope when it's not being used (though if it's a long piece of rope you can get away with merely coiling the ends); if you don't, then the resulting kinks in the rope will diminish its overall strength. Coil rope using both hands. If you're right-handed, support it with your left hand and bring it around clockwise with your right hand, giving it a gentle but firm twist as you go to flatten it out (a coiled rope that's full of "kinks" is no use to anyone). If you're left-handed, reverse the hands and use an counterclockwise coiling motion. Try and make sure the coils are of even length, as this makes them easier to handle and simpler to hang; always hang ropes when you're not using them, rather than laying them on the floor.

To finish off, when you've got about 90–120cm (3–4ft) of rope left, wrap it around the coil three times, then take the end and turn it into a loop. Push the loop through the gap in the top half of the coil and then slip it over the top. Pull the end tight to help flatten the coil of rope. Some people believe that braided rope keeps its strength and shape for longer if you coil it into a figure eight, but with modern rope that's looked after properly, that's not necessary.

The Beaufort Scale

When it comes to wind speed, sailors all over the world share a common language. It's the language that allows them to distinguish between a light air and a gentle breeze, or a fresh breeze and a strong gale. It was invented in 1805 by an admiral in the Royal Navy, Sir Francis Beaufort, and it's named after him to this day. Welcome to the Beaufort Scale.

Force	Velocity	Description
0	Less than 1 knot	Calm: smoke rises straight up in the air and the sea is like a mirror.
1	1–3 knots	Light air: gentle ripples form on the surface, but it's easier to tell the wind direction by watching smoke blow across the water.
2	4–6 knots	Light breeze: you can feel the wind on your face, a weather vane will turn, short wavelets form on the surface, without crests.
3	7–10 knots	Gentle breeze: larger wavelets with some breaking crests, leaves constantly moving in the trees, small flags will blow straight.
4	11–16 knots	Moderate breeze: will blow loose paper off the deck and move small branches in the trees; wavelets become longer, with frequent breaking crests.
5	17–21 knots	Fresh breeze: moderate waves with plenty of whitecaps, small trees sway, and wavelets form on inland waters.
6	22–27 knots	Strong breeze: large waves with extensive white tops form, the large branches of trees move, telephone wires hum, hard to open an umbrella.
7	28–33 knots	Near gale: white tops aplenty as the sea starts to heave, some even breaking up into the air and being blown by the wind; on land, entire trees move and it becomes awkward to walk into the wind.
8	34–40 knots	Gale: moderately high waves with edges that break into spindrift or heavy foam; branches begin to break from the trees and it becomes genuinely hard to walk anywhere because of the wind.
9	41–47 knots	Strong gale: high waves, foam so dense that it begins to make it difficult to see properly; some damage to roof tiles and chimneys.
10	48–55 knots	Storm: very high waves, foam blows even further, making visibility even worse; trees may uproot, and the wind causes minor structural damage.
11	56–63 knots	Violent storm: the waves are now exceptionally high—high enough to conceal a medium-sized ship—and entire areas may appear white; visibility even more reduced; on land, expect widespread structural damage.

10 GETTING HELP

Although you may be stuck, lost or hurt, there's still an awful lot you can do to make sure that you get found long before you're in any danger. As with most things outdoors, the key is to stay calm and focused and then take action. If you've come prepared and you know how to use your gear, you can survive long enough for help to find you.

You will be found. Believe it.

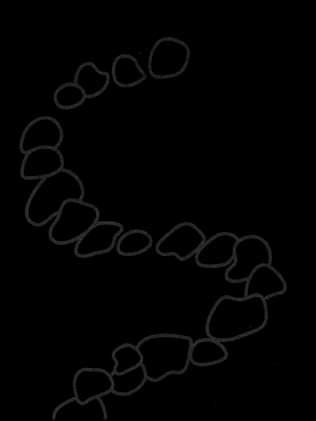

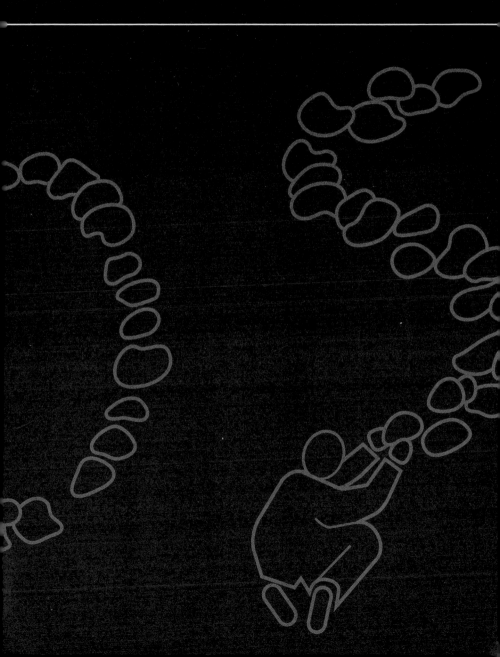

Getting
Ready

Getting
Going

Getting
Stuck

Getting
Lost

Getting
Hurt

Getting
Shelter

Getting
Warm

Getting
Food

Getting
Wet

Getting
Help

First Thoughts

First things first. If you followed the advice at the beginning of the book, told someone where you were going and made arrangements with them to check in, you can rest assured that someone's going to be coming after you. Go back to page 60 and read up on how search parties work. Remind yourself that you shouldn't get downhearted if it's taking longer than you think it ought to. Then come back here and think about the following:

TRY YOUR MOBILE PHONE

When calling from a mobile phone in an emergency, dial 999 in the UK or 112 which is the European emergency number and works everywhere in the EU. In many remote places, of course, you won't get a signal, but it's worth finding some high ground and trying. If the signal is not strong enough for a call, it may be possible to send a text message. The emergency numbers can't receive texts; instead, text a trusted friend or relative and get them to call the emergency number. If you've got a map, you can let them know where you think you are and how you're holding

up. You can also arrange a signal that you can use to attract attention when the search party arrives. Prepare as much information as you can before you make the call or text—phones are unreliable, especially when you need them most.

TRY YOUR WHISTLE

A whistle (assuming you have one) is a powerful thing. It can make a lot more noise than you can, and it carries a long way. You can keep blowing a whistle all day, so it will last much longer than your voice. The universal signal for help is three blasts on the whistle, then wait for ten seconds, then another three blasts, and so on. Repeat this every ten minutes or so. You could also use anything to make a noise—a metal spoon hit against a cooking pot is one idea.

LISTEN

Searchers may respond with a whistle blast or shout of their own. If you're constantly making a racket (or blowing your whistle), you won't hear them.

SHOUT "HELP!"

As with the whistle, shout "Help" three times, but then pause for 20 seconds (you'll need more of a rest); listen for a response. Shout again. Always shout "Help!" to distinguish you from members of the search party, who may also be shouting to each other.

Preparing for Rescue

If you're lucky enough to be found by a search party travelling by foot, then things are going to be pretty straightforward. But what happens if help comes from the air or you are out at sea? There are certain things you need to be prepared for in the event of a rescue that will make your life—and the lives of your rescuers—a lot easier.

KNOWING YOU'VE BEEN SEEN

Unless you've got an emergency radio with you, it may be difficult to know whether or not a search party has actually seen you. Over land, a pilot will usually tip their wings, raising and lowering them in very deliberate fashion to indicate they've spotted you; helicopter pilots will hover and "nod" the aircraft forward and backward. Remember that if an aircraft makes a sign like this but then flies off it could be for any number of reasons—to fetch ground-based help or summon a helicopter; or just to get more fuel. At sea, a ship may sound its horn or signal with a searchlight to indicate you've been found.

CLEAR THE DECKS

On page 155 we'll explain how to use brightly coloured clothing to attract attention. If you use this method and rescue comes from the air, it's very important that you gather up the signal articles before any attempted rescue; anything loose and laying around can easily be sucked into an aircraft engine or get tangled in a helicopter's rotor blades.

DO AS YOU'RE TOLD

Although being spotted by a rescue plane or helicopter is a fantastic thing, it's not the end of the story. In many situations it won't be possible for the aircraft to land in a nice open spot and hang around while you to stroll over and climb inside. Instead, the terrain may be difficult and the weather conditions worse. If that's the case, it's very important that you're able to follow instructions from the rescue team—otherwise you could put your life, and theirs, in danger. In difficult conditions, a helicopter may not able to land and will therefore have to winch you up, perhaps using a "horse collar" or a basket. Always follow the instructions you're given to the letter and don't do anything (for example, try to remove your harness if you think you're safely inside the aircraft) until you're told to.

Getting Ready

Getting Going

Getting Stuck

Getting Lost

Getting Hurt

Getting Shelter

Getting Warm

Getting Food

Getting Wet

Getting Help

Signs for Help

If you don't have any brightly coloured gear you can use, there are other ways you can attract attention—and bear in mind next time you hit the trail that perhaps camouflaged equipment isn't such a cool idea after all.

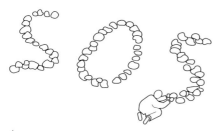

▲
The bigger the sign, the better the chances someone will see it from the air

NATURAL SIGNS

Use whatever materials are available to make big—really big—signs that can be seen from the air. If there are plenty of stones and rocks about, you should spell out "S.O.S." or "HELP", or make large "X" signs on the ground. If you're forced to move on, leave the signs where they are. If you're confident you can choose a direction and actually keep on course, add a large arrow pointing in the direction you're taking. If you don't think you can keep a true course, leave a note instead (see below). Signs can be scratched in surfaces such as sand, gravel, rock and snow. For more signs and signals you can use to attract attention, turn to page 178.

LEAVING A NOTE

It's hardly the height of sophistication, but if you're forced to move, leaving a note can help searchers find you much more quickly. You can only be in one place at one time, but by leaving notes along the way, you greatly increase the search party's chances of finding you. Notes should include a few important details. If you understand maps, leave references and direction indicators;

if not, even "I'm heading towards the big ugly hill with a bald top on it" is better than nothing. Remember to include the date and time on the note, as well as an indication of your general condition.

SIGNS AND BLAZES

When lost and in need of help, remain in the one place. But if you need to move, you can use various signs to let searchers know where you're going. Just keep in mind that there's no guarantee that the people searching for you will understand the signs, so keep things simple. A pile of stones with an arrow pointing in the direction you're travelling is good. So is driving a stick into the ground at an angle, pointing the way you're going, and so is cutting arrows on tree bark with your knife—anything that looks manmade and out of the ordinary and shows the direction in which you're moving will help the searchers.

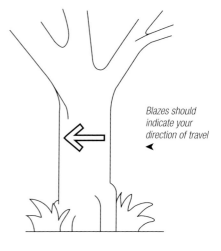

Blazes should indicate your direction of travel
◄

> Tossing green branches onto a burning fire will produce a good smoke signal

Containing your signal fire

It's very important that your fire doesn't get out of control. If it does, it may spread to the surrounding vegetation and become a devastating bushfire. This happens routinely around the world, and many thousands of hectares and hundreds of homes have been destroyed by signal fires that have run riot. The problem is three-fold:

- People light more than one signal fire and they can't control them all sufficiently.
- Fires are often built on higher ground where the wind can blow sparks, embers and other burning material onto nearby bushes and trees.
- Signal fires tend to be larger than campfires and therefore harder to control.

If you are rescued as a result of a signal fire, make every effort to put it out completely before you leave the scene. If it's not possible for you to put out the fire, get your rescuers to help. By the time fire-fighters arrive at the scene, it may be completely out of control.

SIGNAL FIRE

Setting a fire to attract attention is fairly simple. You should site your fire on higher ground or in a clearing—if you're in a heavily wooded area, the smoke will dissipate before it can break through the canopy, and light from the fire simply won't be seen. Remember that you want it to burn brightly at night and smoke a lot during the day. You probably won't want to keep a signal fire going all the time, so have it ready to go whenever you do need it. That means building an easily lit, dry-as-possible fire (see page 106 onwards) and keeping it covered so it stays dry. You'll also need plenty of fuel. Dry sticks and branches will create a bright fire that can be seen easily at night, while adding green branches to an established fire will give off plenty of smoke during the day.

TREE TORCH

This involves deliberately setting fire to a tree that's standing on its own, by piling tinder and kindling between the boughs and lighting it. This kind of fire is very hard to control, and may spread despite your best efforts. It should only be used in a real emergency.

Getting
Ready

Getting
Going

Getting
Stuck

Getting
Lost

Getting
Hurt

Getting
Shelter

Getting
Warm

Getting
Food

Getting
Wet

Getting
Help

Other Ways to Attract Attention

Depending on what you were able to bring with you, there may be other ways you can attract the attention of other people. Bear in mind there will be two kinds of people out there: those looking for you, and those passing by who have no idea you're in trouble. You need to attract the attention of both.

FLARES

Various types are available from good outdoors stores. Safety flares are weatherproof and will give off a good strong glow for about 15 minutes. To really attract attention, though, you need something like a combined flare/launcher, which will hurl a magnesium flare hundreds of metres up where it can be seen for kilometres around, night or day. Choose several small flares rather than one big one—they can be temperamental and refuse to go off just when you need them.

SMOKE CANISTERS OR GENERATORS

These can really help if you need to attract attention and don't have time to start a fire. They usually "burn" for between one and three minutes, depending on which kind you buy and give off a hell of a cloud of smoke. They're less useful in high winds where even thick smoke can get blown away and actually confuse rescuers as to your exact position.

STROBE LIGHTS

These come in all shapes and sizes, from tiny stick-on ones to large, circular lights that would look more at home on the top of a police car. However, they're all good at punching out a bright, hard-to-ignore light that can be seen for kilometres. Look for ones with a once-per-second flash and some means of attaching them to your gear so you can keep your hands free if you need to be doing something else at the same time.

Using a signal mirror

It doesn't have to be a real mirror, of course. Any bright, reflective surface will do the trick. This is one of the most effective ways of attracting attention when the sun is shining, and under the right conditions it can be seen for kilometres. To help you aim the beam in the right direction, place your free hand in the air between the object you're trying to signal and your mirror. Then adjust the mirror so that it's reflecting the sun's light onto your hand. Move your hand away and the light will be directed onto the object. Remember to flash the light on and then off the object in that three-pause-three-pause rhythm. This will attract attention more than just trying to shine a steady beam.

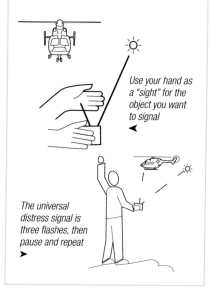

Use your hand as a "sight" for the object you want to signal
◄

The universal distress signal is three flashes, then pause and repeat
➤

This is a tricky one to answer, because it will depend on your individual situation. Generally speaking, if you're unhurt and can move, you should try to set up camp in accordance with the advice on page 91. However, the most comfortable campsite may not be the best place from which to attract attention, especially from the air. Ideally, you should make camp on a gentle slope with a few rocks and bushes for a windbreak, just down from a large clearing on a ridge, near a stream, and so on. Given that your situation is likely to be less than perfect, you should think seriously about making a judgment that balances comfort with visibility.

Look at the gear you've got and see if there's anything there that could be used to attract the attention of anyone— someone flying overhead, walking in the valley below, on the other side of the trees you're using as a windbreak—anyone.

- Survival bags are often brightly coloured and highly visible. Lay the bag out flat on open ground to attract attention from the air, or secure it between trees or over bushes. If the vegetation is very green, any white material will stand out really effectively.
- If you believe rescue will come from the air, spread your gear out during the day and make it as big as possible, so it's easier to see. Remember that geometric shapes like squares are instantly out of place and thus more easily noticed.
- Hiking clothes are often brightly coloured and can be spread on the ground or hung in trees to attract attention. Alternatively, you can tie something brightly coloured—like a T-shirt—to the end of the longest

stick you can find and then wave it in the air. The combination of the bright colours and side-to-side movement is an excellent attention-grabber.
- If you hear an aircraft and don't have a signal fire or a flare or a mirror ready, don't jump up and down waving your arms. Instead lay flat down on the ground in a star shape, as this makes you as big as possible when seen from the air. Move your arms and legs as if you were trying to make a snow angel.
- If you're leaving visual clues like this on a ridge or hill, remember that someone in a plane may be able to see things placed on one side of the ridge, but not the other, depending on which way they fly past. Spread your clues out on both sides if you can.

Getting Ready

Getting Going

Getting Stuck

Getting Lost

Getting Hurt

Getting Shelter

Getting Warm

Getting Food

Getting Wet

Getting Help

Distress Signals at Sea

In the unlikely event that it all goes horribly wrong and you need to attract attention to your plight, there is a range of devices and techniques available to get you noticed. In some situations, this will be as simple as hailing a fellow boat owner as they pass by, or waving at the bloke in the canoe on the other side of the river, but sometimes circumstances will dictate otherwise, and you need to be prepared.

Flares are very bright

FLARES

Flares come packed in waterproof containers with instructions on the side. Regularly check the expiry dates of the flares and replace if necessary. There are basically three types of pyrotechnic signals that can be used in an emergency to attract attention. These are:

Red Hand Flares

Red hand-held flares are designed for use at night, but can also be seen during the day. They can be seen for up to 10km (6.2m). Once ignited, hold the flare away from you and as high as possible until it ends.

Orange Hand Flares

Designed for use during daytime only, these are visible for up to 4 km (2.4m) by observers at sea level and up to about 10 km (6.2m) by aircraft. As for red flares, hold the ignited orange flare as far away from you as possible.

Red Parachutes

These are used to attract attention when help is a long way away. Red Parachutes shoot up to about 300m (1,000ft) and then burn for around 40–60 seconds; in good, clear weather they can be seen up to 40km (25m) away at night and up to 15km (9.3m) away during the day.

What if I don't have anything with me?

If you've been foolish enough to come out without any means of attracting attention, then there's still an internationally recognized cry for help. Stand—very carefully—and face the direction that you expect help to come from; then stretch your arms out on either side to make a T-shape. Slowly raise and lower your arms, keeping them outstretched.

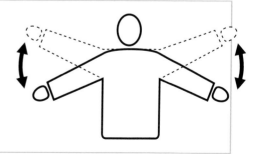

Sheets and Flags

Flags are less visible over a long distance, but they don't "run out". You should be aware of the international maritime signal flags for a vessel in distress: the blue-and-white chequered flag flown together with the horizontal striped (blue, white, red, white, blue) flag—the international signal flags for the letters "N" and "C" respectively. Another sheet/flag that you'll see has a black square and a black circle against an orange background.

EPIRBs

An EPIRB—emergency position indicating radio beacon—is a device that beams your position to rescue services. In many places it is compulsory for vessels over a certain length (e.g. 8m or 26ft) operating more than a certain distance (e.g. 2 nautical miles) from the shore—check your local regulations. In fact, whatever the authorities stipulate, it's a good idea for all vessels venturing offshore to carry one. Once activated, an EPIRB transmits a distress signal for at least 48 hours that can be detected by satellites and aircraft.

Other Methods

- A simple mirror is an amazingly effective signalling device in clear conditions with good sunshine; it's obviously less effective in other circumstances. Hold it by the edges, and aim it in the direction from which you think rescue might be coming, rocking the mirror up and down to produce a regular flash. In perfect conditions, pilots have reported seeing a signal mirror flashing almost 160km (100m) away.
- A foghorn—the modern version can be used to create a series of uniformly long blasts to attract attention.

Flare safety and use

A misfired flare can easily add to your problems rather than coming to your rescue. Flares can start a fire on the boat, or set trees alight if you are firing them from a remote shore where you've had to land; they can set sails on fire, too. The best thing to do is to treat them like firearms—keep them safe and study how to use them properly. Store them in a watertight container, make sure you know where they are, don't point them at anyone, hold them away from your body, and launch them downwind.

Note: Flares should only be used in an emergency. They are not fireworks, and setting them off for fun is not acceptable. A flare tells other sailors and the emergency services that you are in trouble; firing them when you are not in distress is an offence.

QUICK REFERENCE

In the pages that follow you'll find a quick and easy reference section to help with many of the situations that commonly occur outdoors, whether they are life-threatening or merely inconvenient.

Situation — Cold

What to do first:
- If there's a wind, get out of it.
- Put more clothes on. Extra layers will trap air between them and help your body to retain heat.
- Put on a hat. Your head loses heat faster than any other part of your body. Also put on gloves.
- Get under cover—this will also help you retain body heat.
- Always put something between you and the bare ground.
- Light a fire.
- Watch for signs of hypothermia.

More information:
Clothing, pages 14–17; Hypothermia, pages 72–73
Shelter, pages 90–99
Making a fire, pages 106–117

Situation — Wet

What to do first:
- Get out of the wind, even if it's just a slight breeze.
- Change out of your wet clothes and into dry ones if you have them. Any dry clothes will make a difference, even if all you have are dry socks and a spare T-shirt.
- If it's still raining, get under cover and don't get any wetter.
- Try to keep your gear dry as well.
- Light a fire.
- If you've been wet and exposed for a while, watch for signs of hypothermia.

More information:
Clothing, pages 14–17
Hypothermia, pages 72–73
Shelter, pages 90–99
Making a fire, pages 106–117

Situation	Lost

What to do first:
- Accept that you're lost.
- Stay calm. Stay where you are and take stock of your situation.
- Now, can you find yourself—either by using your map or by observing your surroundings?
- Can you backtrack to the last location where you knew weren't lost?
- Contact the emergency services, by phone or use a PLB.
- Unless you're certain you can, stay where you are and make camp.
- Think about how you can make yourself easier to find.
- Stay put unless an emergency forces you to move.

More information:
S.T.O.P., page 54
How rescue teams work, pages 60–61
Finding where you are, pages 56–57

Situation   Out at Night

What to do first:
- Unless you're in danger or there's a medical emergency and you absolutely have to keep moving, you should stop.
- Make camp.
- Make a fire.
- Make yourself comfortable—as long as you're uninjured, an unexpected night out is nothing to worry about.
- If you must move in the dark, stay together if you are in a group—either hold on to each other's hands or rope yourselves together.
- If you're in a group, talk to each other to keep in contact.
- If you're alone, talk to yourself to keep your spirits up.

More information:
Making camp, pages 90–99
Making a fire, pages 106–117
Moving at night, pages 48–49

Situation   Behaving Erratically

What to do first:
- If someone in your party starts behaving oddly, they're probably ill.
- Reassure them and the rest of the group.
- Get them to sit or lay down, depending on how agitated they are.
- Do they suffer from a known medical condition?
- If they have medication, administer it.
- If they don't, be prepared to evacuate them if their condition deteriorates.
- Are they dehydrated?
- Are they hypothermic?
- Are they hyperthermic?
- Have they been drinking alcohol?
- Have they fallen and hit their head?

More information:
Dehydration, pages 74–75
Hypothermia/Hyperthermia, pages 72–73
Shock, page 78
Evacuation, page 79

Situation | Fallen Over

What to do first:
- Is the person conscious and breathing?
- Take control of the situation and reassure them.
- Check for broken bones.
- Check for bleeding.
- Check for severe bruising (which may indicate internal bleeding).
- If they're in shock, lay them down, raise their feet slightly, and keep them covered loosely for warmth.
- Don't give them food or drink.
- Don't attempt to move on until they are clearly recovered.

More information:
Administering CPR, pages 76–77
Checking for fractures, pages 78–79
Signs of shock, page 78
Bleeding, pages 80–81

Situation | Aerial Rescue

What to do first:
- Activate a PLB (if you haven't already) or fire off a flare if you have one.
- Try to signal the aircraft with a mirror or other reflective object.
- Lay on the ground in a star shape and move your arms and legs as if creating a snow or sand "angel." This makes you look as big as possible.
- Use any brightly coloured tent/tarp/plastic sheets to attract attention. Lay them flat on the ground or hang them in trees.
- Prepare a signal fire (bright at night, smoky during the day).
- Make signs from natural materials (i.e. "S.O.S." or "HELP").

More information:
Attracting attention from the air, pages 154–155
Ground-to-air signs, page 178

Situation | Broken Bone

What to do first
- If the injured person is unconscious, check that they are still breathing.
- If they're not breathing, commence CPR.
- If they are breathing, try to locate the fracture while they're still unconscious.
- Check the injured person for internal bleeding.
- When they regain consciousness, reassure them.
- Check for signs of shock.
- Immobilize the limb.
- Either use the splint from your medical kit or improvise one from other materials at hand.
- Remember to cushion the splint so it doesn't rub against the injured limb.
- Don't tie the splint too tight, or it will restrict circulation.

More information:
Administering CPR, pages 76–77
Fractures, pages 78–79
Signs of shock, page 78
Bleeding, pages 80–81

Situation | Can't Make A Fire

What to do first
- Don't panic—there are other ways to get warm.
- Add extra layers of clothing, particularly a hat if you have one.
- Remember that clothes only help you retain heat, so generate more heat by moving around, running on the spot, jumping up and down, and so on.
- Get under cover if you can.
- Even getting inside a large plastic rubbish bag will help you retain heat.
- If you're lying down, remember to have something to insulate you from the cold ground: two plastic rubbish bags with a layer of leaves between them will help.
- When you're warmer, try to light a fire.

More information:
Clothing, pages 14–17
Getting shelter, pages 90–99
Making a fire, pages 106–117
Lighting a fire, pages 112–113
Lighting a fire without matches, pages 114–117

Situation   Bear Trouble

What to do first
- Keep a safe distance—an absolute minimum of 100ft (30m).
  Further away is better still.
- Watch for signs on the trail that indicate you're entering bear country.
- Make a noise on the trail—bears will usually prefer to fade away into the woods.
- If a bear comes toward you, make yourself as big as you can by making sure you've got
  your pack on, opening your jacket, and so on.
- If you're in a group, stay together, as this will make you look bigger and therefore
  less vulnerable.
- If a bear comes into your camp, make a lot of noise to scare it off.
- Remember, it's still unusual for a bear to attack.

More information:
Signs that you're in bear country, page 86
Bear attacks, page 86
Keeping bears out of your camp, page 87

Situation   Can't Purify Water

What to do first
- If it's a choice between going thirsty and drinking untreated water, drink the water.
- Untreated water may make you sick, but it will rarely kill you.
- Many water-borne infections don't display any symptoms for days or weeks.
- Many people can be infected by parasites such as giardia lamblia but never display
  any symptoms.
- Clear running water close to its source will be as safe as you are likely to find.
- Filter out debris with a homemade bandanna-and-sand filter.
- Do NOT drink from a water source that is clearly being used by animals. You could
  become seriously ill.

More information:
Drinking untreated water, page 125
Treating water, pages 126–127

What to do first
- Don't assume you're safe because the storm is far away—a bolt of lightning can be 8km long and carry 100 million volts of electricity.
- Get rid of metal objects and don't stand near anything metal (such as a wire fence or a railway line).
- Don't shelter under a tall tree.
- Put something between you and the ground, such as a foam pad.
- Dark cloud bases and increasing wind are storm signs.
- If you can hear thunder, a lightning strike is possible.
- Your chances of being struck by lightning are low—between 1 in 280,000 and 1 in 700,000, depending on who you believe.

More information:
Lightning strikes, page 45

What to do first
- Reassure the injured person.
- Stop the bleeding.
- Blood from capillaries and veins can usually be stopped by pressing directly down on the wound.
- Spurting blood from an artery may also be stopped by pressing down directly on it, but you may also need to locate the nearest pressure point.
- Check for internal bleeding.
- Elevate the injured limb.
- Clean and dress the wound.
- Check for infection.
- Do NOT use a tourniquet unless you know what you're doing.

More information:
Types of bleeding, page 80
Stopping the bleeding, page 81
Dressing the wound, page 82
Infections, page 82

What to do first
- Short term, use your wet-weather gear or poncho to stay dry.
- Short term, shelter under a tree (unless it looks like lightning).
- Get your tent or tarp up if you're quick enough!
- Note any manmade shelters as you pass them—sometimes it's best to go back to a shelter you know is there, rather than pressing on in worsening conditions in the hope of finding one that might be somewhere ahead.
- Overhangs and caves make good natural temporary shelters.
- Make a natural shelter or windbreak.

More information:
Sheltering under natural features, page 90
Poncho shelter, page 93
Tarp camping, pages 94–95
Building a shelter, pages 98–99

What to do first
- Find north using your compass.
- Find north using a homemade compass.
- Find north using the stars.
- Find north on your map.
- Make your way to higher ground where you can get a better view of what's around you.
- Hold the map out flat in front of you and try to match features on the map with any natural features around you.
- Look particularly for high ground, lakes, rivers and other distinctive natural features.

More information:
Using a map and compass, pages 32–33
How to find yourself again, pages 56–57
How to find yourself without a map or a compass, pages 58–59

What to do first
- Insect and spider bites are generally unpleasant but harmless.
- If you're sitting directly on the ground or a wall, get up and brush yourself off—there may be more.
- If you've been stung by a bee, remove the sting by scraping it off with the edge of your knife. Do NOT use tweezers to pull it out.
- A little antihistamine or antiseptic cream is usually enough to prevent a bite or sting from becoming too angry.
- If you've been bitten by any kind of mammal, you must seek medical attention without delay, because you may contract rabies.

More information:
Bites and stings, page 69

What to do first
- "Listen" to your feet. Act on the first signs of soreness.
- Remember that blisters can sometimes begin as a hot spot on your foot, or even as an itchy area.
- If the blister hasn't actually formed, cover the area with tape or "moleskin" to reduce the friction between the skin and your boot.
- If the blister has already formed, cut a round hole in several layers of moleskin and position it over the blister. This protects the blister and the delicate skin beneath it.
- Don't burst a blister—it's nature's own bandage.

More information:
Blisters, page 67

Situation	Leaving Signs

What to do first
- If you're leaving notes or signs for a search party, make sure they're as unsubtle and as visible as you can make them. Don't think little cutesy twists of grass—think piles of stones.
- Cut blazes on trees or make arrows from sticks to show your direction of travel.
- When leaving a note, make sure you include the time, date, direction of travel, and your condition. That way, if you need special help, rescuers can summon it even before they find you.
- As you travel, remember to blow your whistle, bang something, or shout "Help" at regular intervals using the three-pause-three-pause sequence.

More information:
Signs for help, pages 152–153

Situation	Move or Stay?

What to do first
- If you're stuck or lost, you should move only if you are in danger or there is a medical emergency. Move only as far as you need to be safe.
- If you're unexpectedly stuck but still comfortable, stay put.
- If you're lost but can make yourself comfortable, stay put.
- Staying where you are increases your chances of being found, because you'll be nearer to the place where you were last seen, your original route or the marked trail.
- If you must move, leave signs, blazes or notes to indicate which way you've gone. Include the date and time, as well as your condition, on the note.

More information:
Moving in the dark, pages 48–49
If you must move, pages 62–63
Marking your trail, pages 152–153

Situation	Running Aground

What to do first
- If you've run into sand at low speed you may be able reverse out again.
- If your sails are still up, get them down so you are not pushed further aground by the wind.
- If you've got a centreboard then pull it up as quickly as you can.
- Rocking the boat from side to side may reduce the draught and in some circumstances allow you to drift free.
- Try setting the anchor and using it to pull yourself off; alternatively, wait and see if the rising tide will float you off.

More information:
Running aground, page 136

Situation	Capsizing

What to do first
- Modern dinghies are designed to drain water quickly and are easy to right again.
- Catamarans are almost impossible for a solo sailor to right again—you're better off saving your energy.
- If you're in a sailboat with a centreboard you may be able to climb up over the gunwale and onto the centreboard as the boat goes over.
- Before trying to right a sailboat, cast off the sheets first or you're likely to capsize all over again just when you think you've got her up.
- Don't throw yourself onto the sail as it goes over—you'll probably just sink the mast.

More information:
Capsizing, page 137

Situation	Fire Onboard

What to do first
- Radio for help.
- Get everyone into a life jacket.
- If the fire is small, keep your head down and use your extinguisher to put it out.
- If the fire is spreading, get out—closing doors behind you as you go; if it's an engine room fire, DO NOT open the door to check.
- Get everyone off the boat and into the dinghy or lifeboat.

More information:
Fire onboard, page 139

Situation	Person Overboard

What to do first
- Shout to reassure the person that you know they've fallen in.
- Someone on the boat needs to keep them in sight at all times—once lost, a person overboard is very difficult to find again.
- Turn the boat towards the direction they fell in so the rudder and propeller are pointing away from them.
- Throw them a lifebuoy with an underarm action, aiming slightly upwind.
- Approach them by heading into the wind or waves to stop the boat from drifting into them accidentally.

More information:
Person overboard, page 140

Maritime Radio Stations

Maritime VHF radio uses 57 channels, which are numbered 1–28 and 60–88. Each channel is allocated a different use; for example, ship-to-ship communications, ship-to-air, port safety, international distress calls, emergencies, and so on. This table is a handy guide to the channels and their respective uses.

Channel Number	United Kingdom	United States	Canada	Australia	New Zealand
0	Private, Coast Guard				
1			Public correspondence (ship-to-shore) BC Coast		
2			Public, BC Coast		
3		Illegal for public use	Public, BC Coast/Inland		Boat to Boat—Kawau
4			Ship-to-ship/shore, commercial and safety, BC, and East Coast		Boat to Boat—Tutukak/Raglan
5			Ship movements		
6	Ship-to-ship, ship-to-air		Ship-to-ship, ship-to-air	Distress—ship-to-air	Working—inter-ship
7			General working channel		
8	Ship-to-ship		Ship-to-ship, East and West coasts, Lake Winnipeg	Working—inter-ship	Working—inter-ship
9	Ship-to-ship	Calling, commercial, and non-commercial	Ship-to-air for maritime support, Atlantic, and BC coasts	Pilots, port operations	Port operations
10	Ship-to-ship		Ship-to-air, Search And Rescue and anti-pollution, General working, Atlantic and BC coasts, Great Lakes		Port operations
11			Vessel Tracking System - BC Coast Pilotage		Port operations
12			Vessel Tracking System—BC Coast Port and pilot ops	Port Operations, Vessel Tracking System	Port operations
13	Ship-to-ship	Bridge-to-bridge safety, vessels greater than 65ft (20m) to maintain watch, transmission limited to one watt	Vessel Tracking System—BC Coast, bridge-to-bridge safety	Port Operations, Vessel Tracking System	Inter-ship navigational safety
14			Vessel Tracking System—BC Coast Port and pilot ops		Port operations
15	Ship-to-ship				
16	International distress, safety, and calling	International distress, safety and calling; all VHF-equipped vessels must keep watch	International distress, safety, and calling	International distress, safety, and calling	International distress, safety, and calling
17	Ship-to-ship				Aquatic sports events
18					
19			Canadian Coast Guard working channel		
20				Repeater operations	Continuous weather, Maritime Safety Service
21		US Coast Guard only	Continuous Marine Broadcasts		Continuous weather, Maritime Safety Service
22		US Coast Guard—public working channel			Continuous weather, Maritime Safety Service
23		US Coast Guard only			Continuous weather, Maritime Safety Service
24	UK Search and Rescue Ground-to-air, UK Search and Rescue Team Working Channel				

Channel Number	United Kingdom	United States	Canada	Australia	New Zealand
25					Maritime Radio Working Channel
26					
27					
28					
60					
61		Illegal for public use			
62	UK Search and Rescue Calling and Helicopter Channel, UK Search and Rescue Team Working Channel				Boat-to-boat—Waiheke/Whangaroa
63	UK Search and Rescue Team Working Channel				Boat-to-boat—Manukau
64	UK Search and Rescue Team Working Channel	Illegal for public use			
65			Marine Assistance Working Channel		Boat-to-boat—Coromandel
66					
67	HM Coastguard Search and Rescue			Working Channel, Marine Weather	Maritime Radio Working Channel
68		Non-commercial			Maritime Radio Working Channel
69		Non-commercial		Australian Navy	Maritime Radio Working Channel, Surf life-saving
70	Digital Selective Calling	Digital Selective Calling	Digital Selective Calling	Digital Selective Calling	Digital Selective Calling
71		Non-commercial			Maritime Radio Working Channel
72	Ship-to-ship	Non-commercial ship-to-ship	Ship-to-ship		
73	HM Coastguard Safety Broadcasts			Ship-to-ship	Marinas—working
74	British Waterways Channel (Canal System)			Ship-to-ship	Working—coast-to-ship
75					
76					
77	Ship-to-ship			Ship-to-ship	
78		Non-commercial			
79					
80	Marinas only			Repeater Operations	Coastguard Radio—Working Channel
81		US Government use only		Repeater Operations	Coastguard Radio—Working Channel
82		US Government use only	Canadian Coast Guard working channel		Coastguard Radio—Working Channel
83		US Coast Guard only	Continuous Marine Broadcasts		
84					Coastguard Radio—Working Channel
85	UK Search and Rescue Team Working Channel		Radio Telephone		Coastguard Radio—Working Channel
86					Coastguard Radio—Working Channel
87	Automatic Identification System	Automatic Identification System	Automatic Identification System	Automatic Identification System	Automatic Identification System
88	Automatic Identification System	Automatic Identification System	Automatic Identification System	Automatic Identification System	Automatic Identification System

Glossary

Like most specialist activities, hiking, camping and boating have generated an extraordinary amount of jargon. In this glossary we'll be picking up the terms that are used in the book and one or two others you may come across as you become more experienced. Of course, it's only a primer, as you'll no doubt discover as the world outdoors starts to reveal itself.

Access points—recognized points where the public can reach a track from carparks, main roads and other community facilities.

Access track—a smaller track that branches off the main track or connects it to another track system.

Back country—area away from permanent buildings and paved roads.

Backpack—a bag, sometimes framed, which you wear on your back to carry sleeping, cooking and camping gear for staying out overnight or longer.

Backpacking—a hike that includes at least one overnight stop to make camp, prepare food and so on.

Beaufort Scale—the system invented by Sir Francis Beaufort in 1805 to measure wind strength.

Bilge—an area at the bottom of some boats where water collects; this has to be pumped dry periodically.

Bivy—short for bivouac, a lightweight, waterproof bag that covers a sleeping bag.

Blazes—marks made to indicate a track. Can be a marker of stones, a cut shape in a tree trunk, a painted sign and so on.

Bluff—a steep headland, riverbank or cliff.

Buoy—a manmade floating marker.

Cairn—a mound of rock built next to a track; used to mark the route.

Catamaran—a boat with two hulls, joined in the middle by a frame.

Cleat—an anvil-shaped fitting on a boat or dock, around which a rope can be looped or tied.

Compass—a device that indicates direction relative to the Earth's magnetic poles. Used for navigation.

Contour lines—lines drawn on a topographic map that indicate elevation.

CPR—cardiopulmonary resuscitation, a way of keeping the heart pumping in an emergency situation.

Cramp—when muscles spasm in a contracted state, usually due to lack of water or salt.

Day pack—smaller backpack used for hikes that don't involve an overnight stay.

Dead reckoning—a way of plotting a course on a boat by extrapolating from your last known position.

Dehydration—what happens when you don't drink enough water—your body can't cool itself down when it's hot and can't generate enough heat when it's cold.

Dinghy—either a small utility craft like a rowing boat that's carried by a larger vessel, or a small sailing boat, often used for racing.

Draught—the distance from the surface of the water to the lowest point of the boat (the tip of the keel).

Drip sticks—sticks attached to guy ropes that ensure water running down them doesn't reach your shelter and soak through.

EPIRB— Emergency Position Indicating Radio Beacon. A device usually carried on boats that is activated in emergencies in order to guide rescuers to your position.

Fire drill—a primitive device for making fire.

Fire piston—a hollow tube-and-plunger combo used for lighting tinder by using compression to heat the air inside the tube.

Fire plough—a tool to make fire by "rubbing two sticks together" in an efficient manner.

Fire steel—a small metal rod and scraper that can be used to create a shower of super-hot sparks for starting a fire.

Flash flood—when torrential rain breaks over mountains and runs off into gullies, ravines and canyons; flash floods are extremely dangerous.

Fuzz sticks—dry, dead wood that's part-scraped with a sharp knife to produce a series of curls still attached to the main trunk that will burn more easily.

Galley—the kitchen on board a boat.

Giardia lamblia—parasite that flourishes in wild water sources that causes sickness and diarrhoea.

GPS—Global Positioning System. By using a phone-sized device, it's possible to bounce information off of a network of 24 satellites that orbit the earth twice a day and then calculate your position down to 15–20m.

Ground mat—also called a sleeping mat or pad, this is usually inflatable, packs down into a small roll and acts as an insulating layer between your sleeping bag and the cold ground.

Glossary

Gunwale—the top edge of the side of a boat.

Habitat—an area that provides plants and animals with everything they need to survive—food, water, shelter and so on.

Hairpin—a sharp turn in a track that reverses the direction of travel going uphill. Designed to limit the effects of erosion.

Head—a boat's toilet.

H.E.L.P—Heat Escaping Lessening Posture. A way of retaining body heat when you're in the water.

Hike—a walk in the wild, for the joy of it.

Hull—the body of the boat. A displacement hull ploughs through the water; a planing hull skims across its surface.

Hyperthermia—potentially dangerous condition when the body produces more heat than it's able to release.

Hypothermia—dangerous condition that occurs when the body is losing more heat than it can generate.

Inflatable—any kind of boat that can be blown up and then deflated for easier storage (see also RIB).

Junction—where two tracks join up.

Keel—the boat's central "fin", which is usually weighted with lead and extends down into the water to help stop the boat from tipping over.

Latitude—the location of a place in terms of its position north or south of the equator.

Layering system—a simple way to prevent your body from losing heat by wearing a base layer, an insulation layer, and a windproof, waterproof shell layer.

Leave No Trace (LNT)—educational program that promotes responsible behaviour, designed to limit the impact of anyone who visits the outdoors.

Longitude—the location of a place to the east or west of the meridian at Greenwich, England (0 degrees longitude).

MARPOL—internationally recognized standards for disposing of waste; stands for MARine POLlution.

MMSI—Maritime Mobile Service Identity, a unique number that's transmitted automatically by newer VHF radios and can be used to identify an individual boat.

Moleskin—thick cotton fabric that can be used to prevent blisters.

Mummy sleeping bag—a sleeping bag with a hood, so-called because it makes the occupant—yep—look like an Egyptian mummy.

Orienteering—finding your way around unfamiliar territory using a map and compass.

Pack out—to take out any garbage or waste you accumulate during a hike and dispose of it responsibly.

PLB—Personal Locator Beacon. A device carried by hikers that is activated in emergencies in order to guide rescuers to your position.

Poncho—light, versatile hooded rainwear that leaves your arms free and covers your backpack. Can also be used to make a simple, tarp-style shelter.

Ravine—a deep, narrow gorge or gully, usually caused by water erosion.

RIB—stands for Rigid Inflatable Boat, a boat in which only part of the hull is inflatable. Often known by the trade name Zodiac.

Semaphore—a system of spelling out words using flags.

Sextant—a device used to navigate by the positions of the sun, moon and stars.

Solar still—an improvised method of collecting water by means of a plastic sheet stretched over a hole in the ground.

S.T.O.P.—principle designed to help you pause and take stock of your situation— stands for Sit, Think, Observe and Plan.

Tarp—or tarpaulin, a waterproof sheet with metal rings arranged around the edges that can be used as a simple, lightweight shelter.

Tiller—a lever used to steer a boat by controlling the movement of the rudder.

Topographic map— a map with accurate graphical representation of the physical features in a particular area—contour lines show elevation and other symbols indicate paths, rivers and lakes, woods, buildings and so on.

Trailhead—entrance to a trail, usually from a carpark, road or other public place.

VHF radio—stands for Very High Frequency and is the radio system used by boats for communicating with each other or with the rescue services, receiving weather forecasts and so on.

Air-to-Ground Signals

It's one thing to get found by an air crew when you're lost, quite another to communicate with them. Fortunately, there are commonly recognized signals that can be used to convey basic messages, either using your body (below) or objects at hand (bottom).

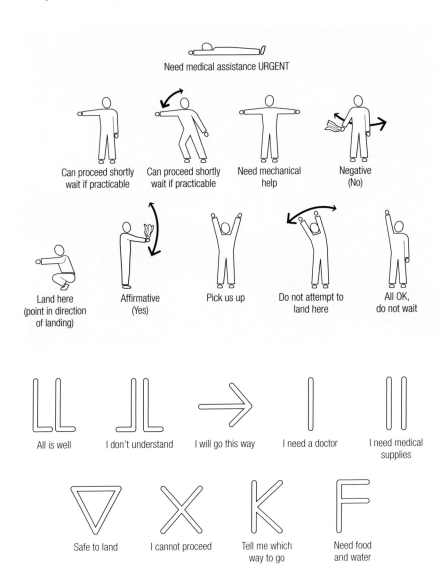

Need medical assistance URGENT

Can proceed shortly wait if practicable

Can proceed shortly wait if practicable

Need mechanical help

Negative (No)

Land here (point in direction of landing)

Affirmative (Yes)

Pick us up

Do not attempt to land here

All OK, do not wait

All is well

I don't understand

I will go this way

I need a doctor

I need medical supplies

Safe to land

I cannot proceed

Tell me which way to go

Need food and water

Conversion Tables

On this page we've put together a set of handy tables to help you convert between various common measurements that are used in relation to area, length, volume and weight, together with the calculation for converting Celsius to Fahrenheit and vice versa.

Area

Metric		Imperial
1 square centimetre	=	0.1550 square inches
1 square metre	=	1.1960 square yards
1 hectare	=	2.4711 acres
1 square kilometre	=	0.3861 square miles
Imperial		Metric
1 square inch	=	6.4516 square centimetres
1 square foot	=	0.0929 square metres
1 square yard	=	0.8361 square metres
1 acre	=	4046.9 square metres
1 square mile	=	2.59 square kilometres

Length

Metric		Imperial
1 millimeter	=	0.0394 inches
1 centimeter	=	0.3937 inches
1 meter	=	1.0936 yards
1 kilometer	=	0.6214 miles
Imperial		Metric
1 inch	=	2.54 centimetres
1 foot	=	0.3048 metres
1 yard	=	0.9144 metres
1 mile	=	1.6093 kilometres

Volume

Metric		Imperial
1 cubic centimetre	=	0.0610 cubic inches
1 cubic decimetre	=	0.0353 cubic feet
1 cubic metre	=	1.3080 cubic yards
1 litre	=	1.76 pints
1 hectolitre	=	21.997 gallons
Imperial (English)		Metric
1 cubic inch (in³)	=	16.387 cubic centimetres
1 cubic foot (ft³)	=	0.0283 cubic metres
1 fluid ounce (fl oz)	=	28.413 millilitres
1 pint (pt)	=	0.5683 litres
1 gallon (gal)	=	4.5461 litres
US measures		Imperial
1 fluid ounce (fl oz)	=	1.0408 UK fluid ounce
1 pint (pt)	=	0.8327 UK pints
1 gallon (gal)	=	0.8327 UK gallons
US measures		Metric
1 fluid ounce (fl oz)	=	29.574 millilitres
1 pint (pt)	=	0.4731 litres
1 gallon (gal)	=	3.7854 litres

Temperature

Celsius to Fahrenheit	(Celsius degrees) x 9/5 + 32
Fahrenheit to Celsius	(Fahrenheit degrees) – 32 x 5/9

Weight

Metric		Imperial
1 milligram	=	0.0154 grains
1 gram	=	0.0353 ounces
1 kilogram	=	2.2046 pounds
1 tonne	=	0.9842 tons
Imperial		Metric
1 pound (lb)	=	0.4536 kilograms
1 stone	=	6.3503 kilograms
1 hundredweight (cwt)	=	50.802 kilograms
1 ton (t)	=	1.016 tonnes
1 square mile	=	2.59 square kilometres

Animal Tracks

On any trek into the bush, even on daytrips in or near cities, you can have lots of fun looking for the signs of passing wildlife, whether they be bird, reptile or mammal. Remember that many national parks run guided tours where they'll tell you more about animal tracks specific to that location and how to spot them.

Hind   Fore

Cat: *average print size 1in approx.*

Crow: *average print size 2.5in approx.*

Deer: *average print size 2.5–3in approx.*

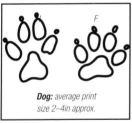

F

Dog: *average print size 2–4in approx.*

H   F

Fox: *average print size 2in approx.*

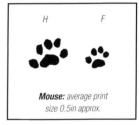

H   F

Mouse: *average print size 0.5in approx.*

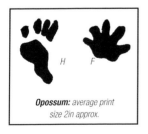

H   F

Opossum: *average print size 2in approx.*

H

F

Rabbit: *average print size (hind) 4in approx.*

Turkey: *average print size 4in approx.*

WHAT TO LOOK OUT FOR

- The weight of an animal directly affects the impression it leaves on the ground—lighter animals leave fainter tracks.
- The ground and its condition affect tracks. It may be more difficult to follow something over hard, dry ground, whereas dusty ground may be better, unless there's wind; marshy ground may be great material for prints but can also fill with water again so they disappear. You get the idea—just be aware that there are pros and cons to all conditions.
- The size of the tracks. It's not just that some animals are larger than others; it's also that many have something distinctive about them. For example, the rear legs and paws of a rabbit are much larger than the front ones.
- The animal's gait—whether it's walking, hopping or running—affects the tracks it leaves. For example, rabbits bound or hop rather than run and this produces a distinct pattern. And there's a differnce between those animals that can retract their claws, like cats, & those who can't, like dogs.

WHERE TO LOOK

For best results, look in places that have little or no vegetation at ground level. Of course, the ground must be soft enough for paw prints to make an impression. Good places to search for tacks include muddy areas, the dust along roadsides, beaches and snow-covered ground.

PRACTISE BEFORE YOU GO

There are plenty of opportunities to apply your skills as a tracker in your own neighbourhood so that you're better equipped when you first go out into the wild. Start with something simple and common like a cat, dog or rabbit and then graduate to those creatures you may meet in the wild. Study their tracks, and after a while you'll begin to understand why they walk as they do and how to spot them in the future.

- Cats have retractable claws, so you won't see any marks from them. The pads on their feet are soft and round, and their toes have plenty of "give," which means the marks they leave are also round. In general, the front paws of a cat are broader, but if these tracks appear all the same size you can tell that a stalking cat is walking in its own footprints.
- Rabbits are easiest of all to spot, with highly distinctive tracks. The main feature is the fact that their hind feet are so much larger than their front ones. And remember that they bound along rather than running evenly.

RESPECTING WILDLIFE

It's worth saying again: animals, birds, insects and plants all live in the outdoors while you are just a visitor—so enjoy yourself, but be respectful.

Many animals are nocturnal, and spotlighting—finding animals with a torch at night—is a popular activity. If you go spotlighting, keep in mind that bright lights can damage animals' eyesight. Use spotlights with protective covers over the lenses. And try not to shine the torch on an animal for more than a minute or so.

Notes and Observations

Notes and Observations

Notes and Observations

Notes and Observations

Notes and Observations

Important Contact Numbers